# Trails to Triumph

Stories We All Need to Hear

*"You reveal the path of life to me; in Your presence is abundant joy; in Your right hand are eternal pleasures."* (Psalm 16:11 HCSB)

## By Curtis E. Nester

Author of
*Faith Will Keep You Afloat*

Copyright © 2012 by Curtis E. Nester

*Trails to Triumph*
by Curtis E. Nester

Printed in the United States of America

ISBN 9781624194382

All rights reserved solely by the author. The author guarantees all contents are original and do not infringe upon the legal rights of any other person or work. No part of this book may be reproduced in any form without the permission of the author. The views expressed in this book are not necessarily those of the publisher.

Unless otherwise noted, Scripture quotations are from the King James Version of the Bible.

Scripture quotations marked HCSB have been taken from the Holman Christian Standard Bible, Copyright © 1999, 2000, 2002, 2003 by Holman Bible Publishers. Used by permission.

www.xulonpress.com

# Dedication

Dedicated to the glory of God, who loved us before we ever loved Him, and sent His Son, Jesus to pay the supreme sacrifice, on the cross, in our place and for our sake. He made it possible for us to have a personal relationship with God, so that we can call him our Heavenly Father, and every broken relationship can be healed.

In memory of my Parents, Cullen Madison Nester and Rachel Boyd Nester, who modeled the Christian life before us. They taught us to love both the Living and the written Word and tried to make sure that our feet were on the right trail.

# Contents

Introduction . . . . . . . . . . . . . . . . . . . . . . . . . . . . .ix
1 - The Path Out of Paradise . . . . . . . . . . . . . . . . 11
2 - Trail to the Unknown . . . . . . . . . . . . . . . . . . . 18
3 - Hesitation Highway . . . . . . . . . . . . . . . . . . . . 25
4 - The Path Up the Mountain . . . . . . . . . . . . . . . 31
5 - The Wilderness Road . . . . . . . . . . . . . . . . . . . 36
6 - A Trail Across the Mountains . . . . . . . . . . . . 43
7 - The Mercy Road . . . . . . . . . . . . . . . . . . . . . . 49
8 - Deserted Highways . . . . . . . . . . . . . . . . . . . . 55
9 - Road to Tomorrow . . . . . . . . . . . . . . . . . . . . . 62
10 - The Road to the Inn . . . . . . . . . . . . . . . . . . . 73
11 - The Road to the Star . . . . . . . . . . . . . . . . . . 83
12 - The Kings Highway . . . . . . . . . . . . . . . . . . . 94
13 - The Road to Everywhere . . . . . . . . . . . . . . 100
14 - Alone Beside the Highway . . . . . . . . . . . . 107
15 - The Road to Jericho . . . . . . . . . . . . . . . . . . 114
16 - Traveling the Same Road Twice . . . . . . . . 120
17 - The Road Less Traveled . . . . . . . . . . . . . . 128
18 - The Cross Road . . . . . . . . . . . . . . . . . . . . . 134
19 - On the Road Again . . . . . . . . . . . . . . . . . . 145
20 - Road to the Light . . . . . . . . . . . . . . . . . . . . 153
21 - The Path Back to Paradise . . . . . . . . . . . . . 160

# Introduction

TRAILS TO TRIUMPH is about *roads* in the Bible and the people who traveled them. In these pages are stories of people who chose their path and followed it for better or worse. Some found tragedy, others pursued a trails that led them to triumph over adversity.

Palestine, the land of the Bible, is situated on a land bridge that connects the continents of Africa, Asia, and Europe. Though the ancient roads were mostly unimproved trails, when the Romans conquered the area they built finely engineered roads, some of which are in existence today. Because these good roads existed and because the Roman military made travel safer, people traveled all over the Roman Empire. This made possible the spread of the Gospel to the far corners of the earth.

A lot of time and research has gone into exploring the background of each story in this book. In some cases I have used imagination to make these stories more vivid, and yet remain true to the facts as set forth in the Bible. I have used the words *trails, paths, roads,* and *highways* interchangeably. Sometimes these are used in their literal sense and lead to a physical destination. At other times they are used as metaphors for a person's direction in life. Each road leads to a different destination, with either good or bad results: *"There is life in the path of righteousness, but another path leads to death."* (Proverbs 12:28 HCSB).

The wise person will carefully choose the road he travels for it determines his ultimate destination. Hopefully, this book will be an encouragement to its readers and motivate them to also read the Bible and be inspired by its message. *"Shew me thy ways, O LORD; teach me thy paths."* (Psalm 25:4 KJV)

# 1

# The Path Out of Paradise

*"In the sweat of thy face shalt thou eat bread, till thou return unto the ground; for out of it wast thou taken: for dust thou art, and unto dust shalt thou return."* (Genesis 3:17-19)

A man and his wife stand outside the gates of a beautiful garden. They cannot go back - the gates are locked - reentry is barred to them. Their only alternative is to go forward. Ahead of them lies the desert, its monotonous surface broken only by sand, rocks and an occasional patch of thorny scrub. Already, they miss the pleasant coolness they had enjoyed in the shade of the garden. The heat is stifling; the air filled with dust. No longer is there a soft carpet of grass beneath their feet. No more gentle breezes carrying the music of birdsong. No longer will food be for the taking by simply stretching out the hand and plucking it from a vine or a tree. A growing thirst reminds them that, now, they must search for water; they must forage for food and dig in the earth to plant seed for harvest. From this point on, their life will be filled with toil.

Somehow, they manage to survive in this strange and difficult world, outside of the paradise which had formerly been their home. Somewhere, they find fertile ground; perhaps a well watered valley, where they can raise crops to support themselves. They learn how to cultivate the land. They learn how to build shelter and make clothing as protection from the weather.

As time passed, they became a family. A son was born to them and they named him Cain, meaning *spear*. He became a tiller of the ground, a farmer. He cultivated, planted and harvested. Later, they had another son, who was given the name of Abel, meaning *vapor*. He became a herdsman, a shepherd. He raised and tended a flock of animals.

Then, when they were grown, the brothers brought offerings to God. Cain offered the fruits of the ground, while Abel made an offering from his flock. Abel's offering was accepted, while Cain's was not. Jealousy rose up in Cain and he killed his brother, while they were out in the field. The New Testament gives us the reason for his despicable act: *"Not as Cain, who was of that wicked one, and slew his brother. And wherefore slew he him? Because his own works were evil, and his brother's righteous."* (1 John 3:12 ).

Abel's life was cut short, but he was not forgotten. He is mentioned in the New Testament, in the eleventh chapter of Hebrews (God's Faith Hall of Fame). *"By faith Abel offered unto God a more excellent sacrifice than Cain, by which he obtained witness that he was righteous, God testifying of his gifts: and by it he being dead yet speaketh."*. (Hebrews 11:4 )

Adam and Eve had been the perfect pair - made for each other. They were created by the hand of

God, in His image. He gave them a perfect paradise in which to live. *"And the LORD God took the man, and put him into the garden of Eden to dress it and to keep it. And the LORD God commanded the man, saying, Of every tree of the garden thou mayest freely eat: But of the tree of the knowledge of good and evil, thou shalt not eat of it: for in the day that thou eatest thereof thou shalt surely die."* (Genesis 2:15-17 ) They enjoyed fellowship with God; and could speak directly to Him and He to them. There was only one restriction, one fruit which they must not eat. As long as they obeyed God, they could live forever.

But they disobeyed. Sin is simply disobedience, transgression of God's law. It begins with doubt. Someone doubts that God really desires the best for his life. Then, it progresses to unbelief; doubting that God will do what He says. The outcome of this is not only an act, but a lifestyle that is contrary to God's will and purpose for one's life. Eve was led into disobedience by the serpent, Satan. Adam did not resist, but followed her into disobedience. Both shared in the guilt.

How could they do such a thing? How could they throw away an ideal life? People still do things which defy common sense, today, when they choose to yield to temptation. The tactics Satan used in tempting Adam and Eve are still in use in our time. They never change and still lead people to do things that destroy their lives. Here is the line of attack Satan employed in the garden:

He began by Casting Doubt on God's Word- *"Now the serpent was more subtil than any beast of the field which the LORD God had* *made. And he said unto the woman, **Yea, hath God said**, Ye shall not eat of every tree of the garden?"* (Genesis 3:1 )

Then, he Contradicted God's Word- *"And the serpent said unto the woman, **Ye shall not surely die**"* (Genesis 3:4 )

Next, he Appealed to the Pride of Life- *"For God doth know that in the day ye eat thereof, then your eyes shall be opened, and **ye shall be as gods**, knowing good and evil."* (Genesis 3:5 )

Finally, the Lust of the Flesh took over- *"And when the woman saw that the tree was good for food, and that **it was pleasant to the eyes**, and a tree **to be desired to make one wise**, she took of the fruit thereof, and did eat, and gave also unto her husband with her; and he did eat."* (Genesis 3:6 )

Adam and Eve had set their feet on the path of disobedience, that leads away from God. Their disobedience brought an immediate consequence. They were cast out of the Garden of Eden and the entrance was barred with a flaming sword. They would know the curse of hardship and death, *". . . cursed is the ground for thy sake; in sorrow shalt thou eat of it all the days of thy life; Thorns also and thistles shall it bring forth to thee; and thou shalt eat the herb of the field; In the sweat of thy face shalt thou eat bread, till thou return unto the ground; for out of it wast thou taken: for dust thou art, and unto dust shalt thou return"* (Genesis 3:17b-19 )

Their sin also brought long-term consequences. When they fell, all of creation was affected. We live in a fallen universe. Perfection is gone; replaced by imperfection and a natural tendency to rebel against God. As descendants of Adam and Eve, we are all born with this sinful nature and the trend is downward, not upward.

But, thankfully, the story doesn't end there. In pronouncing the curse, God also offered the hope of a Redeemer, who would bruise Satan's head. *"And I will put enmity between thee and the woman, and between thy seed and her seed; it shall bruise thy head, and thou shalt bruise his heel."* (Genesis 3:14-15 )

The Promised Redeemer is Jesus:

*And so it is written, The first man Adam was made a living soul; the last Adam was made a quickening spirit. Howbeit that was not first which is spiritual, but that which is natural; and afterward that which is spiritual. The first man is of the earth, earthy: the second man is the Lord from heaven. As is the earthy, such are they also that are earthy: and as is the heavenly, such are they also that are heavenly. And as we have borne the image of the earthy, we shall also bear the image of the heavenly.* (1 Corinthians 15:45-49)

MILEPOSTS-

**The Wrong Road never leads to the Right Place-**
There are many paths in life, but, as Adam and Eve discovered, God's way is the only one which

leads to happiness and eternal life. All other paths lead away from God and away from paradise. *"There is a way which seemeth right unto a man, but the end thereof are the ways of death."* (Proverbs 14:12 )

**The Situation is Never Hopeless-** After the death of Abel, God gave Adam and Eve another son, Seth, who represented a new beginning and the rebuilding of their family. Seth fathered a son named Enos and the Bible says that *". . . then began men to call upon the name of the LORD."* (Genesis 4:26b )

**There is Life after Death-** Adam and Eve brought sin and death into the world. God sent Jesus to bring eternal life to all who believe, *"For as in Adam all die, even so in Christ shall all be made alive."* (1 Corinthians 15:22 )

**Where was the Garden of Eden located?-** The only thing the Bible tells us concerning the Garden of Eden's location is found in Genesis 2:10-14, "A river watering the garden flowed from Eden; from there it was separated into four headwaters. The name of the first is the Pishon; it winds through the entire land of Havilah, where there is gold…The name of the second river is the Gihon; it winds through the entire land of Cush. The name of the third river is the Tigris; it runs along the east side of Asshur. And the fourth river is the Euphrates." The exact identities of the Pishon and Havilah rivers is unknown, but the Tigris and Euphrates rivers are well known.

## The Path Out of Paradise

If the Tigris and Euphrates mentioned are the same rivers by those names today, that would put the Garden of Eden somewhere in the Middle East, likely in Iraq. It cannot be mere coincidence that the Middle East region is where the planet was most lush—the place where the Garden of Eden was placed. If oil is, as most scientists believe, primarily decayed vegetation and animal matter that has decomposed, then this is the area where we might expect the greatest deposits of the substance we call oil. Since the Garden was the epitome of perfection, it stands to reason that the decomposition of the earth's most perfect and lush organic materials would produce vast stores of the earth's best oil.

People have searched for the Garden of Eden for centuries to no avail. There are various locations that people claim to be the original location of the Garden of Eden, but we cannot be sure. What happened to the Garden of Eden? The Bible does not specifically say. It is likely that the Garden of Eden was completely destroyed in the Flood or that it lies decomposing into oil buried beneath centuries of sand deposits.

(© Copyright 2002-2009 Got Questions Ministries- Used by permission from the website- www.GotQuestions.org)

# 2
# Trail to the Unknown

*". . . and he went out, not knowing whither he went."* (Hebrews 11:8b)

A caravan moves along a trail that follows the central mountain ridges southward toward Canaan. The view from the ridge is spectacular. To the west, the Coastal Plain stretches all the way to the blue haze over the Great Sea. To the east, the land drops sharply into the Jordan Valley. It is a part of the Great Rift Valley, which stretches from Lebanon all the way down through Palestine and into Africa. It runs through the lowest point on earth, near the Dead Sea. The caravan consists of Abraham, his wife, Sarah, his nephew, Lot, their servants, herds of camels, cattle, and flocks of sheep. They are following a trail into the unknown.

Abraham and his entourage have come from the city of Haran (or Charran), which means "road." Located between the Tigris and Euphrates rivers, in what is today Turkey, it was on the trade route from Damascus. Terah, Abraham's father had migrated there from Ur, in Mesopotamia. In those days, the Persian Gulf extended inland all the way to Ur, and

## Trail to the Unknown

it was a great metropolitan seaport that grew wealthy from business and trade. A temple, the Ziggurat, was built there, patterned after the Tower of Babel. Abraham's family were probably traders and Abraham, himself, was not just a nomadic herdsman, but a man of great wealth and power.

Our story began 2,000 years after Adam, and 400 years after Noah's Flood, when most of mankind had forgotten God. Many had degenerated into idolatry, worshiping carved images and the forces of nature. The city of Haran was known for its worship of the moon god, and some of Abram's relatives had become part of the cult. But Abram, whose name meant "Exalted father," still worshipped the One True God. God appeared to him, calling him to leave his homeland and go to a place He would show him. His name was changed to Abraham, "Father of Multitudes."

*Now the LORD had said unto Abram, Get thee out of thy country, and from thy kindred, and from thy father's house, unto a land that I will shew thee: And I will make of thee a great nation, and I will bless thee, and make thy name great; and thou shalt be a blessing: And I will bless them that bless thee, and curse him that curseth thee: and in thee shall all families of the earth be blessed. So Abram departed, as the LORD had spoken unto him; and Lot went with him: and Abram was seventy and five years old when he departed out of Haran. And Abram took Sarai his wife, and Lot his brother's son, and all their substance that they had gathered, and the souls that they had gotten in Haran; and they went forth to go into the land of Canaan; and into the land of Canaan they came. And Abram passed through the land unto the place of Sichem, unto the plain of Moreh. And the Canaanite was then in the land.* (Genesis 12:1-6)

Today, we know that part of the world as a dry, almost desert-like area, with few trees, but in Abraham's day it was covered with forests, extending from the Cedars of Lebanon down through Canaan. There were three major routes through Canaan: the Way of the Philistines which ran along the coastal plain, the Ridge Route which passed through the central mountains, and the Kings Highway which ran through the Jordan Valley. Following the Ridge Route, Abraham arrives at Sichem (or Shechem) which means "shoulder". It was located on a shoulder of the mountains, between Mount Gerizim and Mount Ebal. There, streams flow from numerous springs down the slopes of the valley. It has been referred to, by travelers to the Holy Land, as a place of surpassing beauty. There, Abraham pitched his tent and built an altar under the oak of Moreh. Then, God appeared to him again, *"And the LORD appeared unto Abram, and said, Unto thy seed will I give this land: and there builded he an altar unto the LORD, who appeared unto him."* (Genesis 12:7). This is part of God's covenant, which he made with Abraham.

The next stop on Abraham's journey was a mountain east of Bethel ("house of God") where he again built an altar to worship God. This time, the Bible says that he *called on the name of the Lord*. This was not a private prayer but a public proclamation. Abraham was telling others, or preaching to them about God. Later, Jacob, Abraham's grandson would return to Bethel many times to seek guidance from God.

Leaving Bethel, Abraham continued southward to the Negeb ("dry or desert"). Later, when famine struck, he took his family to Egypt. When they arrived there, Abraham was afraid that the men would kill him and take Sarah. This is something that is still practiced in the Middle East. Sarah is referred to as a woman of fair countenance and she would have been attractive to the men of Egypt, so, Abraham told everyone that she was his sister. She actually was his half-sister, being the daughter of Terah , who had more than one wife. As Abraham had feared, when Pharaoh heard of Sarah's beauty he had her brought to his palace, intending to make her his wife. But, God sent a plague on Pharaoh and when he discovered the truth, he returned Sarah to Abraham and sent them away.

They returned to Hebron in the land of Canaan. Abraham and his family did not settle for long in one place but moved periodically to find grazing and water for his flocks. His nephew, Lot and his family were living in the same area. When their livestock multiplied to the point that there was not enough grass for both, their herdsmen quarreled. In an effort to avoid strife, Abraham proposed that they separate and offered Lot the choice of which territory he would take. Lot, seeing that the land of the Jordan Valley was well-watered, chose that and eventually settled in Sodom. His choice turned out to be disastrous for his family. (To see what happened read Chapter 3 **Hesitation Highway**)

While sitting in the shade of his tent in the plains of Mamre one day, Abraham saw two men approaching. He greeted them and entertained them with the usual Eastern hospitality, by serving them a meal of butter, milk, and meat. Then they made a startling announcement.

*And he said, I will certainly return unto thee according to the time of life; and, lo, Sarah thy wife shall have a son. And Sarah heard it in the tent door, which was behind him. Now Abraham and Sarah were old and well stricken in age; and it ceased to be with Sarah after the manner of women. Therefore Sarah **laughed** within herself, saying, After I am waxed old shall I have pleasure, my lord being old also?* (Genesis 18:10-12)

Later, when Sarah did indeed have a son, they named him Isaac ,which means *Laughter*. (For an exciting event in the life of Isaac see Chapter 4 **The Path Up the Mountain**.)

Abraham's faith had faltered, while in Egypt, as he resorted to trying to protect himself with a half-truth rather than trusting God to take care of the situation. Yet, in spite of his shortcomings, Abraham's life was characterized by faith which was tested and proved many times, and he is referred to as "the Father of the Faithful."

MILEPOSTS-

**The Promises to Abraham-** God spoke to Abraham many times during his life and made a number of promises to him. Included in these promises, were three very important things: (1) That Abraham and his descendants would inherit the land of Canaan, (2) That his descendants would become a great Nation, and (3) That through Abraham's descendants, all Nations would be Blessed.

**The Faith of Abraham-** *"By faith Abraham, when he was called to go out into a place which he should after receive for an inheritance, obeyed; and he went out, not knowing whither he went. By faith he sojourned in the land of promise, as in a strange country, dwelling in tabernacles with Isaac and Jacob, the heirs with him of the same promise: For he looked for a city which hath foundations, whose builder and maker is God."* (Hebrews 11:8-10)

**The Righteousness of Abraham-** was due, not to his personal goodness, but as a result of his faith. *For what saith the scripture? Abraham believed God, and it was counted unto him for righteousness.* (Romans 4:3). The way of salvation is not by one's good works, but by Grace through Faith. It is a Gift from God.

**Greater than Abraham-** Abraham, like all men, had his weaknesses and sometimes failed to trust God completely for everything. Because of the weakness and failures of men, God sent One greater than Abraham to be the Savior of mankind. The leaders of the Jews once asked Jesus, "*Art thou greater than our father Abraham, which is dead? and the prophets are dead: whom makest thou thyself?*" (John 8:53) When Jesus replied that He knew Abraham, they followed this up with: *". . . Thou art not yet fifty years old, and hast thou seen Abraham? Jesus said unto them, Verily, verily, I say unto you, Before Abraham was, I am."* (vs.8:57b-58)

# 3

# Hesitation Highway

*". . . Escape for thy life; look not behind thee, neither stay thou in all the plain; escape to the mountain, lest thou be consumed."* (Genesis 19:17)

A father, his wife, and their two daughters rush along the road that stretches from their city to the mountains surrounding the valley. The place they are running away from is a prosperous, well populated city, located on the southeastern side of the "Salt Sea." It is one of five cities situated in a well-watered and fertile plain, with abundant crops and a wealth of minerals. The family is in a hurry to escape the disaster that is about to fall upon this area. Four of the five cities are going to be destroyed by a rain of fire. Having been warned of the imminent annihilation, these four people are fleeing for their lives. And yet, one of their number, the wife, hesitates. Remembering the home that they are leaving behind, she stops and does the very thing she was warned not to do. She turns around, lingers and looks back toward the city they have just fled. It is a fatal mistake. Fiery projectiles are already pelting down and she is soon covered with a molten mixture of tar, sulfur and salt. Her husband and two daughters have no other option than to continue their flight. Even a moments delay would have been fatal. The next day, as the sun rose, they entered the little the town of Zoar, which was outside the range of destruction. They found shelter there, temporarily, but later proceeded along the same road to their original destination, the mountains. This mountain road, along with some of the cities, has since been lost under the spreading waters of the sea.

Their narrow escape is the result of choices made earlier. The father, whose name is Lot, is the nephew of Abraham. Their families had lived together in the region until their numbers increased to the point that the land was unable to sustain them. They needed to put some distance between their flocks. When Abraham offered Lot his choice of land, he chose the best grazing land, which was in the plain south of the Salt Sea. *"And Lot lifted up his eyes, and beheld all the plain of Jordan, that it was well watered every where, before the LORD destroyed Sodom and Gomorrah, even as the garden of the LORD, like the land of Egypt, as thou comest unto Zoar. Then Lot chose him all the plain of Jordan; and Lot journeyed east: and they separated themselves the one from the other. Abram dwelled in the land of Canaan, and Lot dwelled in the cities of the plain, and pitched his tent toward Sodom."* (Genesis 13:10-12)

Notice that the plain of the Jordan is referred to as being like *the garden of the Lord*, or the Garden of Eden. There were five cities located in the Plain: Sodom, Gomorrah, Zoar, Admah and Zeboim. They were well off, but they drifted into such a grievous, sinful lifestyle that their scandalous reputation came to the attention of God. He sent angels to investigate and deal with the situation. They visited Abraham and, when he learned that the cities were going to be destroyed, he pled with God to spare them if as few as ten righteous people could be found. But there were not even ten righteous people in the cities. Only Lot and his family, out of the thousands of inhabitants, would be spared. The angels visited Lot and warned him to flee the impending destruction. Lot and his family were slow to respond and had to be forcibly led out of the city.

*And it came to pass, when they had brought them forth abroad, that he said, Escape for thy life; look not behind thee, neither stay thou in all the plain; escape to the mountain, lest thou be consumed. And Lot said unto them, Oh, not so, my Lord: Behold now, thy servant hath found grace in thy sight, and thou hast magnified thy mercy, which thou hast shewed unto me in saving my life; and I cannot escape to the mountain, lest some evil take me, and I die: Behold now, this city is near to flee unto, and it is a little one: Oh, let me escape thither, (is it not a little one?) and my soul shall live. And he said unto him, See, I have accepted thee concerning this thing also, that I will not overthrow this city, for the which thou hast spoken. Haste thee, escape thither; for I cannot do any thing till thou be come thither. Therefore the name of the city was called Zoar. The sun was risen upon the earth when Lot entered into Zoar. Then the LORD rained upon Sodom and upon Gomorrah brimstone and fire from the LORD out of heaven; And he overthrew those cities, and all the plain, and all the inhabitants of the cities, and that which grew upon the ground. But his wife looked back from behind him, and she became a pillar of salt.* (Genesis 19:17-26)

In the twentieth century, archaeologists discovered the sites of five ancient cities on the east side of the Dead Sea. Charred wooden beams, and burnt bricks have been found in the area, along with a layer of ash up to 20 inches deep. There are deposits of salt, sulfur, and bitumen (tar & hydrocarbons) in the region. Scholars speculate that when God pronounced judgment upon the cities, the bitumen was ignited and molten sulfur and salt were thrown into the air. When Lot's wife stopped to look back at the burning cities, she was caught in a virtual rain of fire and brimstone. Burned and suffocated to death, she became encrusted with a layer of sulfur and salt, turned into a literal "pillar of salt."

The destruction of the Cities of the Plain serve as a warning to all who reject God's Word and live without regard to any limitation upon their fleshly desires. *"Even as Sodom and Gomorrha, and the cities about them in like manner, giving themselves over to fornication, and going after strange flesh, are set forth for an example, suffering the vengeance of eternal fire."* (Jude 1:7)

In the New Testament, Jesus was questioned about when the Kingdom of God would come. He replied:

*Just as it was in the days of Noah, so it will be in the days of the Son of Man: people went on eating, drinking, marrying and giving in marriage until the day Noah boarded the ark, and the flood came and destroyed them all. It will be the same as it was in the days of Lot: people went on eating, drinking, buying, selling, planting, building. But on the day Lot left Sodom, fire and sulfur rained from heaven and destroyed them all. It will be like that on the day the Son of Man is revealed. On that day, a man on the housetop, whose belongings are in the house, must not come down to get them. Likewise the man who is in the field must not turn back. Remember Lot's wife!* (Luke 17:26-32 HCSB)

Extreme immorality and wickedness are the hallmarks of the times in which Noah and Lot lived. Most people continued to live their lives as though nothing was wrong. They either ignored the wickedness of their culture or condoned it. The similarities with our age are striking. Perversion is being exalted as "normal" behavior. Killing the unborn is called a "right." And, if anyone summons the moral courage to speak out, then they may be subject to prosecution for "hate crimes." The majority of people are just too busy going about their lives to become alarmed or try to change their culture.

MILEPOSTS-

**Remember Lot's Wife-** Mrs. Lot was so near to being saved, but she loved Sodom so much that she couldn't resist the temptation to turn back for one more look. Many people, today, are fascinated by the world and unable to resist temptation. *"Love not the world, neither the things that are in the world. If any man love the world, the love of the Father is not in him. For all that is in the world, the lust of the flesh, and the lust of the eyes, and the pride of life, is not of the Father, but is of the world. And the world passeth away, and the lust thereof: but he that doeth the will of God abideth for ever."* (1 John 2:15-17)

**Make a Commitment to God-** Don't hesitate or halt between two opinions, but dedicate your life to living for God. Be a part of the solution, not part of the problem. *"That ye may be blameless and harmless, the sons of God, without rebuke, in the midst of a crooked and perverse nation, among whom ye shine as lights in the world"* (Philippians 2:15)

**Be Ready for the Lord's Return-** *Likewise also as it was in the days of Lot; they did eat, they drank, they bought, they sold, they planted, they builded; But the same day that Lot went out of Sodom it rained fire and brimstone from heaven, and destroyed them all. Even thus shall it be in the day when the Son of man is revealed. In that day, he which shall be upon the housetop, and his stuff in the house, let him not come down to take it away: and he that is in the field, let him likewise not return back.* (Luke 17:28-31)

# 4

# The Path Up the Mountain

*"In the mount of the LORD it shall be seen..."* (Genesis 22:14a)

It has been three days since they began their journey. A man, his son, and two servants travel along the trail that leads northeast toward a mountain sixty miles from their home. The servants are leading donkeys, one loaded with wood. The father is preoccupied, turning over in his mind a command he has been given. It puzzles him because it seems inconsistent and contradictory. God had told Abraham to take his son, Isaac, and offer him as a sacrifice on Mount Moriah. Isaac is the son through whom God had promised descendants as numerous as the stars in the sky, and through whom all the world would be blessed. Surely, Abraham's God would not require human sacrifice, as the pagans did. Finally, he resolves in his mind to obey God and leave the outcome to Him. At the foot of the mountain, Abraham says to his servants, *". . . Stay here with the donkey. The boy and I will go over there to worship; then we'll come back to you."* (Genesis 22:5b HCSB). Notice that Abraham said "**we** will come back to you." He didn't understand what was happening, but he maintained a steadfast faith that, somehow, God would work it all out.

As they were climbing up the mountain - the very same mountain where one day the Jewish Temple would be built - Isaac, puzzled at the absence of a lamb, asked about the apparent omission, *". . . And he said, Behold the fire and the wood: but where is the lamb for a burnt offering?"* (Genesis 22:7). Abraham's answer demonstrates his faith that God would provide a way, *"And Abraham said, My son, God will provide himself a lamb for a burnt offering: so they went both of them together."* (Genesis 22:8)

When they arrived at the place where God had directed them to go, Abraham built an altar, and arranged the wood on it. Then, after tying Isaac up, he placed him on top of the wood. Now, Isaac was not a child, he was a grown man. He could have overpowered his father, who was well-advanced in years, and escaped. Instead, he submitted to his father. Over a thousand years later, Jesus would submit to the will of His Father and offer Himself as the supreme sacrifice for our sins. *"And being found in fashion as a man, he humbled himself, and became obedient unto death, even the death of the cross."* (Philippians 2:8)

As Isaac lay, stretched out on the wood, Abraham took a knife and lifted it up, in preparation to slay his son. He must have wondered *why* and *for what purpose* did God ask him to do this? Isaac too, must have had troubling thoughts about why his life should be required as a sacrifice. As Abraham raised the knife in his trembling hand, he heard a voice from heaven, saying, *". . . Lay not thine hand upon the lad, neither do thou any thing unto him: for now I know that thou fearest God, seeing thou hast not withheld thy son, thine only son from me."* (Genesis 22:12)

It was then, that Abraham caught sight of a ram entrapped in a thicket of brambles. He took the ram and offered it as a burnt offering in place of Isaac. *"And Abraham called the name of that place Jehovahjireh: as it is said to this day, In the mount of the LORD it shall be seen."* (Genesis 22:14). The words Jehovah-jireh literally mean *the Lord will see to it*, or *the Lord will provide*. Many years hence, God did "see to it" and provided a perfect Lamb, the Lord Jesus, as a sacrifice for our sin, on the cross. The site of His crucifixion was on a hill, which was a part of the same mountain where a substitute was provided for Isaac.

Abraham was tested and he passed the test. He did not question God. He trusted God in a situation where he could not understand the reasons nor the outcome. *"By faith Abraham, when he was tried, offered up Isaac: and he that had received the promises offered up his only begotten son, Of whom it was said, That in Isaac shall thy seed be called: Accounting that God was able to raise him up, even from the dead; from whence also he received him in a figure."* (Hebrews 11:17-19) Immediately after this, God confirmed His covenant with Abraham to make his descendants as the stars of the sky, and again promised that through them all the nations of the earth would be blessed.

The offering of Isaac is a "type" or picture of Jesus' death on the cross. Here are just a few of the ways that it prefigured the sacrifice of Christ:

1. For the three days they traveled toward the mountain, Isaac was as good as dead in the mind of Abraham. Jesus was three days and nights in the tomb after His death on the cross.
2. Isaac did not resist, but submitted to the will of his father, just as Jesus would submit to the will of His Father.
3. Isaac carried the wood for sacrifice. Jesus carried His cross to Calvary.
4. God provided a substitute sacrifice for Isaac, just as Jesus was our substitute. *"He that spared not his own Son, but delivered him up for us all, how shall he not with him also freely give us all things?"* (Romans 8:32)

MILEPOSTS-

**Trials or Temptations?-** Satan uses **Temptations** to bring out the **Worst** in us. God uses **Trials** to bring out the **Best**. *"No one undergoing a trial should say, "I am being tempted by God." For God is not tempted by evil, and He Himself doesn't tempt anyone."* (James 1:13 HCSB)

**When You are Tested-** Remember this advice from the book of Proverbs: *"Trust in the LORD with all thine heart; and lean not unto thine own understanding."* (Proverbs 3:5)

**God's Purposes-** God works in ways that are mysterious to us, in accomplishing His purposes. The reasons may be beyond our comprehension at present but, someday, we will understand just what God was doing in our lives. An old hymn expressed it this way:

*"Farther along we'll know all about it, Farther along we'll understand why"*.

**Sacrifice-** Sacrifice is the surrender of one's will to God. That is, not insisting on your own way, but accepting God's way. In the Garden of Gethsemane, Jesus prayed, *"Saying, Father, if thou be willing, remove this cup from me: nevertheless not my will, but thine, be done."* (Luke 22:42)

# 5

# The Wilderness Road

*I am like a pelican of the wilderness: I am like an owl of the desert.* (Psalm 102:6)

Early in the morning, as they were waking up, the Hebrew families, looked out their tent doors and discovered that the ground had turned white. Every bush around their camp was covered with a white crystalline blanket. It looked like a heavy frost. They did not know what it was and asked *"what is it?"* using the Hebrew word *mawn*, which literally means "what is it?" So the mystery substance became known as *manna*.

> *And when the dew that lay was gone up, behold, upon the face of the wilderness there lay a small round thing, as small as the hoar frost on the ground. And when the children of Israel saw it, they said one to another, It is manna: for they wist not what it was. And Moses said unto them, This is the bread which the LORD hath given you to eat.* (Exodus 16:14-15)

Moses told them it was the bread which God had given them to eat and instructed them to take only what each family needed for that day. If they took more, what was left over would spoil. But, on the sixth day, they were to take enough for that day plus enough for the Sabbath. Miraculously, it kept overnight and did not spoil, so they had enough food without working on the Sabbath. There have been many "naturalistic" explanations for manna, but these are inadequate. The provision of the manna was a miracle and its preservation over the seventh day confirms the miracle. The manna could be baked or boiled, so there was some variety in their meals.

In the New Testament, Jesus said that He was the living bread which came down from heaven and that those who partook of Him would live forever, *"This is that bread which came down from heaven: not as your fathers did eat manna, and are dead: he that eateth of this bread shall live for ever.* (John 6:58)

The Israelites began complaining from the very beginning of their exodus, *". . . For it had been better for us to serve the Egyptians, than that we should die in the wilderness."* (Exodus 14:12b) They continued to complain as they journeyed toward the Promised Land, sorely trying the patience of Moses and God. Their continual complaining and failure to act on faith would ultimately have dire consequences.

Continuing their journey, they were led to Mount Sinai, where they received God's Law, dealing with their relations with God and with people. They spent about a year at Mount Sinai, receiving the law and organizing themselves for worship and conquest. Leaving Sinai, they marched 150 miles through the wilderness to Kadesh-barnea. From the time they had fled from Egypt, it took them about 18 months to reach Kadesh, on the southern border of the promised land, but their journey was far from over. As we will see, it took them much longer to actually enter into Canaan.

From Kadesh, they sent twelve spies, one for each tribe of the Israelites, into Canaan to reconnoiter, in preparation for conquest of the land. Returning after 40 days, the spies brought with them fruits from the land, figs, pomegranates and a cluster of grapes so large that it took two men to carry. Ten of the spies gave a negative report, saying, *"And there we saw the giants, the sons of Anak, which come of the giants: and we were in our own sight as grasshoppers, and so we were in their sight."* (Numbers 13:33) Only two of the spies, Joshua and Caleb, had the perspective of faith:

*And Joshua the son of Nun, and Caleb the son of Jephunneh, which were of them that searched the land, rent their clothes: And they spake unto all the company of the children of Israel, saying, The land, which we passed through to search it, is an exceeding good land. If the LORD delight in us, then he will bring us into this land, and give it us; a land which floweth with milk and honey. Only rebel not ye against the LORD, neither fear ye the people of the land; for they are bread for us: their defence is departed from them, and the LORD is with us: fear them not.* (Numbers 14:6-9)

But the Israelites were not in the mood to trust God for their future. They chose to believe the negative report, *"All the Israelites complained about Moses and Aaron, and the whole community told them, "If only we had died in the land of Egypt, or if only we had died in this wilderness!"* (Numbers 14:2). Because of their unbelief and unwillingness to enter the Promised Land, God gave them what they asked for. They were sentenced to wander for 40 years, a year for each day that the spies had been in Canaan, until all of the adult population died in the wilderness.

*Then the LORD spoke to Moses and Aaron: "How long must I endure this evil community that keeps complaining about Me? I have heard the Israelites' complaints that they make against Me. Tell them: As surely as I live, declares the LORD, I will do to you exactly as I heard you say. Your corpses will fall in this wilderness—all of you who were registered in the census, the entire number of you 20 years old or more—because you have complained about Me. I swear that none of you will enter the land I promised to settle you in, except Caleb son of Jephunneh and Joshua son of Nun. I will bring your children whom you said would become plunder into the land you rejected, and they will enjoy it. But as for you, your corpses will fall in this wilderness.* (Numbers 14:26-32 HCSB)

The account of their 40 years of wandering in the wilderness is contained in the book we call Numbers.

The Hebrew name for this book is Bamidbar, which means *In the wilderness*. During those years, the people continued to murmur, complain and grumble. They did not stay on the move all the time, but would camp at different places for a while, then move on. Moses had to endure their murmuring and complaining all that time. Yet, he was constantly interceding with God, on their behalf. He exhibited great faith and endurance during this time of hardship. Remember, he had spent 40 years, previously, in the wilderness, tending the flocks of his father in law, Jethro. He had learned his lessons well.

Forty years later, all the Israelites who left Egypt have died, with the exception of Moses, Joshua, Caleb, and the children who had been under twenty years of age when their parents had refused to enter Canaan. Now, they turn, and once more begin to march toward the promised land. The Israelites, however, appear to have inherited the complaining ways of the previous generation. They begin to complain, as their parents did, about their hardships and even about the Manna that God had given them for food. *"And the people spake against God, and against Moses, Wherefore have ye brought us up out of Egypt to die in the wilderness? for there is no bread, neither is there any water; and our soul loatheth this light bread."* (Numbers 21:5).

In response, God sent fiery serpents among them. When many of them were bitten and dying, the people came to Moses and said, *". . . We have sinned, for we have spoken against the LORD, and against thee; pray unto the LORD, that he take away the serpents from us. And Moses prayed for the people."* (Numbers

21:7). God commanded Moses to make a serpent of bronze and place it on a cross shaped pole. Anyone who was bitten, if they looked at it, would live.

The serpent represented *sin*, and bronze represents *judgment*. Ever since the Garden of Eden, mankind has been beguiled by that old serpent, Satan. The bite of sin brings both physical and spiritual death. But God has not left us without a remedy. *"And as Moses lifted up the serpent in the wilderness, even so must the Son of man be lifted up: That whosoever believeth in him should not perish, but have eternal life."* (John 3:14-15) Our sin was judged on the cross of Jesus. When we believe in Him, our sin is forgiven and we are healed of the fatal bite of sin.

MILEPOSTS-

**Daily Bread -** There was a lesson in the manna. By giving the Israelites only one day's supply at a time, God was teaching them that they needed to rely on Him for their daily needs. In the New Testament, Jesus taught us to pray, *"Give us this day our daily bread."* We need to seek His face and worship Him each day and not depend just on Sunday's worship to meet all our spiritual needs. You can't fill up your tank one day and then run all week on that.

**Faltering Faith -** The Christian life is not a fifty-yard dash, but a marathon. Many make a good beginning, but fall by the wayside when the going gets tough. God delivered the Israelites from slavery and brought them to the border of the Promised Land. It was theirs; it had been given to them, but they could not just walk in and settle down. They would be required to conquer it. At the critical moment, when they saw the opposition, their faith faltered. They had the faith to begin, but not to finish. We are not promised an easy life, but: *"We know that all things work together for the good of those who love God: those who are called according to His purpose."* (Romans 8:28 HCSB)

**The Ten or the Two -** When the twelve spies came back from exploring Canaan, ten recommended against trying to conquer it. Two, Joshua and Caleb, were sure that with God's help, they would be victorious. The majority is not always right. Living for God means swimming against the stream of humanity. It means, often, being unpopular, but God's way is always best.

**Wandering in the Wilderness -** The Israelites aren't the only ones who have had to spend years wandering in a wilderness. When we go against God's will for our lives, we will wander in a spiritual wilderness until we repent and turn back into the way He has prepared for us. Someone has said, "Sin will always take you farther than you meant to go, and keep you longer than you meant to stay."

# 6

# A Trail Across the Mountains

*"I will lift up mine eyes unto the hills, from whence cometh my help. My help cometh from the LORD, which made heaven and earth."* (Psalm 121:1-2)

An 85 year old man stands looking out over the mountains. The green hills are fertile and watered with springs which flow down the mountain sides and across the valley. This is an area inhabited by fierce giants, who live in walled cities. It will not be easy to drive them out, but this man, in spite of his age, is still strong and ready to face the challenge. He has been faithful, when others doubted. He has endured many years in the wilderness. Now, as one of the last two survivors of his generation, he is prepared to do whatever it takes to possess the land that had been promised to him 45 years ago. He has proven his faith and courage through all the years of hardship. He has followed a long trail, which now has led him to this mountain. So, he makes his request, *"Now give me this mountain"*.

*Then the sons of Judah came to Joshua in Gilgal. And Caleb, the son of Jephunneh the Kenizzite, said to him, You know the thing that Jehovah said to Moses the man of God in Kadesh-barnea regarding you and me. I was forty years old when Moses the servant of Jehovah sent me from Kadesh-barnea to spy out the land. And I brought him word again as it was in my heart. But my brothers that went up with me made the heart of the people melt; yet I fully followed Jehovah my God. And Moses swore on that day, saying, Surely the land on which your feet have trodden shall be your inheritance, and your sons' forever because you have fully followed Jehovah my God. And now, behold, Jehovah has kept me alive these forty-five years as He said, even since Jehovah spoke this word to Moses, while Israel wandered in the wilderness. And now, lo, I am eighty-five years old today. As yet I am as strong today as I was in the day that Moses sent me. As my strength was then, even so is my strength now, for war, both to go out and to come in. And now give me this mountain of which Jehovah spoke on that day. For you heard in that day how the giants were there, and that the cities were great and fortified. If Jehovah will be with me, then I will be able to drive them out, as Jehovah said. And Joshua blessed him, and gave Hebron to Caleb the son of Jephunneh for an inheritance. And Hebron became the inheritance of Caleb, the son of Jephunneh the Kenizzite, to this day, because he fully followed Jehovah, the God of Israel.* (Joshua 14:6-14)

Caleb had been 40 years old when Israel first reached the goal of their exodus from Egypt. They could have moved into the Promised Land, but they let fear defeat them. Only Joshua and Caleb had the faith to believe that, with God's help, they could conquer and inhabit the land of Canaan. It had been promised to Abraham and his descendants. The time to enter into the land was at hand but the majority faltered in unbelief. On the threshold of victory, they turned back and a whole generation would never see that land again, with the exception of Joshua and Caleb:

*We came to the land where you sent us, and surely it flows with milk and honey. And this is the fruit of it. However, the people that dwell in the land are strong, and the cities are walled, very great. And also we saw the children of Anak there. The Amalekites dwell in the land of the south, and the Hittites, and the Jebusites, and the Amorites dwell in the mountains. And the Canaanites dwell by the sea and by the coast of Jordan. And Caleb stilled the people before Moses and said, Let us go up at once and possess it. For we are well able to overcome it. But the men that went up with him said, We are not able to go up against the people, for they are stronger than we. And they brought up an evil report of the land which they had searched to the sons of Israel, saying, The land through which we have gone to search it, is a land that eats up those who live in it. And all the people whom we saw in it were men of stature. And there we saw the giants, the sons of Anak, of the giants. And we were in our own sight like grasshoppers, and so we were in their sight.* (Numbers 13:27b-33)

One of the cities Caleb received was Hebron, located southwest of Jerusalem, in a valley, at an elevation of 3,000 feet above sea level. North of Hebron lies the Plain of Mamre, where Abraham camped when he first came to Canaan. It was here that God made a covenant with him, promising to make of him a great nation, and that through his descendants all nations would be blessed. Here, he pled with God to spare Sodom if there were as few as ten righteous people in the city; then he watched the smoke of its burning as fire and brimstone fell from the sky. Later, it was in the plains of Mamre where God appeared to Abraham and told him that he would father a son in his old age. When she heard this, Sarah laughed because she was old. In due time, the son was born and he was named Isaac, which means "laughter".

When Sarah died, Abraham purchased a cave in the field of Machpelah to bury her in. It became the burial place of many of the Old Testament Patriarchs, including Abraham and Isaac. Joseph traveled from Egypt to bring the body of his father, Jacob, to be buried at Machpelah. Then when Moses led the Hebrews out of Egypt, in the Exodus, they carried the bones of Joseph with them to be buried in the same place. In the age of the monarchy, King David ruled Judah from Hebron for 7 years. Eventually, he was anointed as king over all Israel, which he ruled from Jerusalem for 33 years.

For Caleb to possess Hebron and the mountain he had been promised required long and difficult warfare. However, he did not lack courage or stamina. He did conquer and possess his land, driving out the fierce giants that had inhabited it. Afterward, his daughter, Achsah, came to see him, and she had a request of her own: *". . . As she got off her donkey, Caleb asked her, "What do you want?" She replied, "Give me a blessing. Since you have given me land in the Negev, give me the springs of water also." So he gave her the upper and lower springs."* (Joshua 15:18b-19 HCSB) The land he had given her was in the Negev (desert), so she needed water in order to make use of the land. Caleb freely gave her what she requested. In that, he was responding in a manner like that of our Heavenly Father; He delights to give good things to His children, and does not withhold his blessings from the faithful.

MILEPOSTS-

**Defeating Your Giants-** Caleb had to defeat the giants who inhabited the land before it was truly his. There are giants in your life, which must be overcome. The giants are whatever comes between you and fellowship with God. They have to be conquered by relying on His power, not your own. Anything else leads to defeat. Six times in the Old Testament it is said of Caleb, *"he wholly followed the Lord."*

**Don't Pray for an Easy Task-** Rather, pray for strength. When God makes a promise He gives us the strength to see it through. When you rely on God's strength, age makes no difference. Caleb climbed his mountain and defeated his giants at the age of 85.

**Caleb's Faith-** Faith is *not* looking on the bright side, as in positive thinking. Faith is *not* believing that everything is going to work out. Faith *is* believing in God, believing His Word, and then *acting* on that faith.

**The Endurance of Faith-** Caleb waited 45 long years to receive the answer to his prayer. When we pray, we must remember that God works in His own time and in His own way. The answers to prayer are often surprising and surpass anything we could have imagined. The saints of old are an example for us to follow: *"Wherefore seeing we also are compassed about with so great a cloud of witnesses, let us lay aside every weight, and the sin which doth so easily beset us, and let us run with patience the race that is set before us, Looking unto Jesus the author and finisher of our faith; who for the joy that was set before him endured the cross, despising the shame, and is set down at the right hand of the throne of God. "* (Hebrews 12:1-2)

# 7

# The Mercy Road

*"The name of the LORD is a strong tower: the righteous runneth into it, and is safe."*
(Proverbs 18:10)

On the flat roofs of their houses, the inhabitants sat, enjoying the coolness of the evening breezes, a welcome break from the heat of the day. Visible across the plain of Mamre, the mountains thrust their peaks toward the clouds. Gradually, the house-top sitters became aware of a figure moving at a rapid pace in the distance. It was a runner, something they had seen on many occasions. The man was obviously in a great hurry. As he came closer, his face revealed extreme agitation, while he constantly glanced backward over his shoulder. He ran like his life depended on it, as it certainly did.

Nod's heartbeat pounded in his ears, as panting for breath, he kept his pace as fast as he could. He was soaked with sweat; he was growing tired, but dared not stop to rest. He only slowed a little, to catch his breath at each crossroads, where he glanced at the signs to make sure he was staying on the right course. The road carried him between the green clad hills and beside the waving crops on the plain. He was thankful that the way was level, with no hills to climb and no rivers to wade. It had been planned this way, to enable those seeking refuge to gain safety without obstacles in their way.

At last, exhausted and almost ready to give up hope, Nod paused to catch his breath. When he looked up he saw the walls which surrounded his goal. With renewed hope, he ran to the gate of the city of Hebron. As he pounded on the gate, he nervously glanced once more, back the way he had come. His pursuer, now close enough to be visible, was coming on at an alarming rate.

Slowly the gates opened and Nod pled his case. He had been cutting wood with a neighbor, and the head of his axe had flown off, striking his neighbor, leaving him dead. It was no fault of his own. It was an accident, but his neighbor's family would seek vengeance upon him. He knew that his only hope of safety lay in getting to one of the "Cities of Refuge". The inhabitants of Hebron grabbed him and pulled him inside the city walls. As the gate closed, the thud of arrows could be heard, striking the gate. He was safe; he had just made it to sanctuary. His pursuer, disappointed at not being able to wreak his vengeance, slowly turned about and headed back to his home.

When Israel conquered and settled the Promised Land, they had been instructed to build six cities, three on either side of the Jordan river. On the East of the Jordan, there were Bezer, Ramoth-gilead, and Golan. On the West side were Hebron, Shechem, and Kedesh. These were designated as "Cities of Refuge".

*Then the LORD spoke to Joshua, "Tell the Israelites: 'Select your cities of refuge, as I instructed you through Moses, so that a person who kills someone unintentionally or accidentally may flee there. These will be your refuge from the avenger of blood. When someone flees to one of these cities, stands at the entrance of the city gate, and states his case before the elders of that city, they are to bring him into the city and give him a place to live among them. And if the avenger of blood pursues him, they must not hand the one who committed manslaughter over to him, for he killed his neighbor accidentally and did not hate him beforehand. He is to stay in that city until he stands trial before the assembly and until the death of the high priest serving at that time. Then the one who committed manslaughter may return home to his own city from which he fled.'" So they designated Kedesh in the hill country of Naphtali in Galilee, Shechem in the hill country of Ephraim, and Kiriath-arba (that is, Hebron) in the hill country of Judah. Across the Jordan east of Jericho, they selected Bezer on the wilderness plateau from Reuben's tribe, Ramoth in Gilead from Gad's tribe, and Golan in Bashan from Manasseh's tribe. These are the cities appointed for all the Israelites and foreigners among them, so that anyone who kills a person unintentionally may flee there and not die at the hand of the avenger of blood until he stands before the assembly.* (Joshua 20:1-9 HCSB)

The Law as given to Moses by God, recognized the sanctity of human life. The murderer must be punished: *"Whoso sheddeth man's blood, by man shall his blood be shed: for in the image of God made he man."* (Genesis 9:6). To prevent the land from being polluted by innocent blood, however, provision was made to protect those who might be involved in accidentally taking a life. That was the reason for the Cities of Refuge. The accused could flee to one of these cities, where he would be safe until a hearing could establish his guilt or innocence. If he was found guilty, he would forfeit his own life. If he was declared innocent, he would be safe from reprisal by the victim's family. But, he had to remain in that city until the death of the current High Priest, living the life of an exile.

Even a stranger in the land could find shelter in one of these cities. The *mercy road* was open to the Jew and Gentile, alike. The roads had to be kept open and be well marked. Once a year, workers were sent to repair the roads and remove any obstacle that might be in the path. Signposts were set up at every intersection, bearing the Hebrew word *Miklac*, which means "refuge" so there would be not difficulty in finding the way.

In the Cities of Refuge we see God is just but also merciful. He has provided a refuge for the sinner. Though guilty and deserving death, *"For the wages of sin is death; but the gift of God is eternal life through Jesus Christ our Lord."* (Romans 6:23), the sinner can find the Way, plainly marked in God's Word, to flee to Jesus, where he can find forgiveness, cleansing, and eternal life: *"There is therefore now no condemnation to them which are in Christ Jesus, who walk not after the flesh, but after the Spirit."* (Romans 8:1)

**Note:** I chose Nod for the runners name because Nod means *fugitive* in Hebrew.

MILEPOSTS-

**The Dangerous Devil-** Just as the avenger sought to kill the runner, Nod, in the story above, so Satan seeks to destroy everyone he can: *"Be sober, be vigilant; because your adversary the devil, as a roaring lion, walketh about, seeking whom he may devour:"* (1 Peter 5:8)

**The Delightful Difference-** God is not seeking to destroy people, but to save them: *". . . As I live, saith the Lord GOD, I have no pleasure in the death of the wicked; but that the wicked turn from his way and live. . . "*(Ezekiel 33:11a)

**Our Refuge is in God-** There is only one place of safety: *"I will say of the LORD, He is my refuge and my fortress: my God; in him will I trust."* (Psalm 91:2)

**Help in time of Trouble-** *"God is our refuge and strength, a very present help in trouble."* (Psalm 46:1).

**Justice is when someone receives what he Deserves-** God is just and cannot just overlook the guilt of sin. The sin debt must be paid.

**Mercy is Not receiving what you deserve-** God is merciful, giving His Son to pay our sin debt.

**Grace is receiving something you Don't deserve-** By grace, He gives eternal life to all who repent, and receive his gift of salvation, made possible through the death of His Son on the cross: *"For he hath made him to be sin for us, who knew no sin; that we might be made the righteousness of God in him."* (2 Corinthians 5:21)

# 8

# Deserted Highways

*". . . the highways were unoccupied, and the travellers walked through byways. The inhabitants of the villages ceased, they ceased in Israel, until that I Deborah arose, that I arose a mother in Israel."* (Judges 5:6b-7)

The sun has set and twilight is drawing a mantle of darkness over the country side. As the light fades, a figure moves from its hiding place in a ravine and creeps stealthily toward the roadway. It is an Israelite, bowed under the burden he carries over his shoulder. Reaching the border of the road he turns and scans his surroundings to make sure that he has not been observed. Then, hastily crossing the road, he descends the other side and quickly conceals himself among the tall grass growing at the edge of the field. It is well that he did, for the muffled sound of hoof beats on the dusty road break the evening silence. He watches as Canaanite soldiers, laughing and joking above the noise of clattering spears and clomping hooves, ride past his hiding place.

As soon as they have moved out of sight, Ishbak rises and resumes walking across the field.

He moves slowly, always wary of being spotted by the marauding enemy. He is weary, but has had a good day of gleaning for food in out of the way corners. Now, he is on his way home with his sack to feed his family for yet another day. These are sad and dangerous times for Israel. Since the days of Joshua, they have not completed the conquest of the Promised Land, but have settled down among the inhabitants, and many have adopted the false gods of the Canaanites. They have forgotten God and, as a consequence, are suffering a miserable existence. Without any real leaders, it is every man for himself in the land: *"In those days there was no king in Israel, but every man did that which was right in his own eyes."* (Judges 17:6)

As Ishbak ekes out his miserable existence, in a country that has forsaken the God of its Fathers, he fervently hopes that Yahweh will send another deliverer for the people. In the past, there had been Judges, or military leaders, who had delivered Israel from its oppressors. Othniel had defeated Mesopotamian invaders. Ehud had assassinated the King of the Moabites. And Shamgar had killed 600 Philistines with an ox goad. After each victory, Israel had peace for a few years. But, then the cycle of sin, suffering and deliverance would be repeated.

It has now been twenty years since a judge has arisen in Israel and things are in a sorry state. The Canaanites patrol the highways and raid the Israelite's fields, destroying their crops. People have abandoned their villages and are now living in caves and strongholds in the mountains. The roads are no longer safe to travel and have fallen into disuse. The

Israelites have been disarmed and have no weapons with which to defend themselves. There is no one to lead in overthrowing their oppressors. The only person whose judgment the Israelites trust is the prophetess Deborah. But what can a woman do?

Deborah, whose name in Hebrew means *Bee*, is the wife of Lapidoth. She lives between Ramah and Bethel in mount Ephraim and is referred to as a *mother in Israel* because of her concern for the people. Without a strong national leader, the people have no one to turn to for help, except her. The Israelites come to her, as she sits under a palm tree, to seek her advice in settling their disputes.

Their land is controlled by the Canaanite king, Jabin, whose army is well equipped with seasoned warriors and iron chariots, under the leadership of a commander named Sisera. When the people, in their distress, cry out to God for help, He hears them and uses Deborah to rally the people to take back their land. Deborah sends for a warrior, Barak or *Lightning*, and says to him,

> *... Hath not the LORD God of Israel commanded, saying, Go and draw toward mount Tabor, and take with thee ten thousand men of the children of Naphtali and of the children of Zebulun? And I will draw unto thee to the river Kishon Sisera, the captain of Jabin's army, with his chariots and his multitude; and I will deliver him into thine hand.* (Judges 4:6b-7)

Barak does not lack courage, but he is reluctant to meet a strong army with untrained men whose only weapons are bows and arrows, slings and stones, and farm implements. They will be outnumbered by superior forces. Since Deborah is the one who has spoken God's prophecy to him, he says he will go to face Sisera's army only if she will go with him. To this, she replies,

> *... I will surely go with thee: notwithstanding the journey that thou takest shall not be for thine honour; for the LORD shall sell Sisera into the hand of a woman. And Deborah arose, and went with Barak to Kedesh. And Barak called Zebulun and Naphtali to Kedesh; and he went up with ten thousand men at his feet: and Deborah went up with him.* (Judges 4:9b-10)

The victory, then, will belong to a woman, not a man. It seems logical that the woman referred to is Deborah, herself, but she isn't named. Who is the woman who will credited with the victory over Sisera?

Barak sends out a call to arms and 10,000 men answer the call. Barak marches his forces northward, across the Jezreel valley to mount Tabor. True to her word, Deborah the prophetess goes with him. Stationed on the slopes of mount Tabor, they keep a watch for the approach of the enemy.

Between mount Gilboa and mount Tabor, the Jezreel valley stretches from the mountains of Samaria to the Mediterranean sea. Thirty miles long and fifteen miles wide, watered by the Kishon river and having fertile soil, it is referred to as the *Breadbasket of Israel*. On its southwest side is the plain of Megiddo, or Armageddon, which someday, will be the scene of the last, great battle on earth (Revelation chapter 16).

When he hears of the gathering of an Israelite army, Sisera comes out with his men and his chariots to the Kishon river, intending to annihilate Barak and his forces.

*And they shewed Sisera that Barak the son of Abinoam was gone up to mount Tabor. And Sisera gathered together all his chariots, even nine hundred chariots of iron, and all the people that were with him, from Harosheth of the Gentiles unto the river of Kishon. And Deborah said unto Barak, Up; for this is the day in which the LORD hath delivered Sisera into thine hand: is not the LORD gone out before thee? So Barak went down from mount Tabor, and ten thousand men after him.* (Judges 4:12-14)

There is someone else in this fight, however: *"And the LORD discomfited Sisera, and all his chariots, and all his host, with the edge of the sword before Barak; so that Sisera lighted down off his chariot, and fled away on his feet."* (Judges 4:15). God sends a fierce storm, that floods the valley, turning it into a marsh. Sisera's chariots become mired in the mud. He has lost his advantage; the Israelites destroy his army and he runs away on foot.

Barak pursues Sisera, who flees to the encampment of Heber the Kenite, a former ally, thinking that he can hide there. As he approaches, he is met by Heber's wife, Jael, who tells him to go into her tent, gives him milk to drink and covers him up. Then, when he has fallen asleep, Jael picks up a tent peg and, with a hammer, drives the peg through Sisera's head until he is pinned to the ground and dies. So, the final victory belongs not to Barak, nor even to Deborah, but to a gentile woman, Jael.

Following the battle, Deborah wrote the *Song of Deborah*, in which she describes the defeat of Sisera: *"They fought from heaven; the stars in their courses fought against Sisera. The river of Kishon swept them away, that ancient river, the river Kishon. O my soul, thou hast trodden down strength*." (Judges 5:20-21).

Then Deborah, a *mother in Israel*, describes the mother of Sisera waiting in vain for his return, *"The mother of Sisera looked out at a window, and cried through the lattice, Why is his chariot so long in coming? why tarry the wheels of his chariots?* (Judges 5:28)

For the next forty years, Israel lived in peace because God used a woman to challenge and inspire the men to rise up and trust God to give them deliverance.

**Note:** The name Ishbak means "one who is empty or exhausted"

MILEPOSTS-

**God has a purpose for your life-** Have you found it yet? Or are you stumbling around in confusion, like

Barak? You will never be happy, nor contented, outside of God's will.

**God uses the unlikely-** Deborah, a woman, was used of God to call the nation to rise up and defeat its enemies. Barak, though reluctant, at first, because he saw the might of Sisera and the weakness of his own army, finally surrendered to God's plan for his life.

> *"But God hath chosen the foolish things of the world to confound the wise; and God hath chosen the weak things of the world to confound the things which are mighty" (1 Corinthians 1:27)*

**When a nation forgets God-** It is already on the road to decline and fall. Our nation is declining with alarming speed because it has forgotten God and has excluded Him from the public square. Pray that the people of our nation will come back to God before it is too late.

# 9

# Road to Tomorrow

*"Return unto thy rest, O my soul; for the LORD hath dealt bountifully with thee."* (Psalm 116:7)

Three women, one older and two younger, walk the well-worn road, followed by their donkey which is laden with all their possessions. They are traveling northward across the treeless limestone plateau that we know today as the trans-Jordanian highlands. The plains are brown this time of year but at the edge of the river Arnon, grass and trees still grow, providing a welcome respite from the heat. When they reach the river, the women pause to rest and their conversation turns to their present condition and the reasons they are making this journey.

The older woman is Naomi and the two accompanying her are her daughters-in-law. Several years before, Naomi (*Pleasant*) and her husband, Elimelech (*My God is King*) had left Bethlehem fleeing a famine. They had settled in the land of Moab, where there was abundant rain and plenty of food. Their two sons, Mahlon and Chilion married Moabite women, Orpah and Ruth. In the passing of time, Elimelech and both sons died, leaving these three women widows. Bereft of her husband and sons, Naomi had heard that the famine in Bethlehem was over, so she decided to return home where she will be among friends and relatives.

As they rest, Naomi talks with her daughters-in-law and tries to persuade them to return to their homes. She reasons that there, they will be among people and customs they know. Both women are devoted to Naomi and protest that they will stay with her. Finally, however, one of the women, Orpah is persuaded to turn back and, amid many tears, she leaves to go back to her parent's home. Ruth, however has been influenced by the faith of Naomi and is not dissuaded but vows to stay with her. Her reply to Naomi is one of the most beautiful expressions of loyalty in the Old Testament:

*And they lifted up their voice, and wept again: and Orpah kissed her mother in law; but Ruth clave unto her. And she said, Behold, thy sister in law is gone back unto her people, and unto her gods: return thou after thy sister in law. And Ruth said, Intreat me not to leave thee, or to return from following after thee: for whither thou goest, I will go; and where thou lodgest, I will lodge: thy people shall be my people, and thy God my God: Where thou diest, will I die, and there will I be buried: the LORD do so to me, and more also, if ought but death part thee and me. When she saw that she was stedfastly minded to go with her, then she left speaking unto her.* (Ruth 1:14-18)

The river Arnon, where they are resting is the northern border of Moab, which was named after one of the sons of Lot, who fled Sodom during its destruction and settled in this land. At this point, the river flows in a declivity only a few feet below the surrounding land. Farther west it drops sharply down through a canyon to the Dead Sea, 1385 feet below sea level. We do not know what route they followed, but it could have been the ancient King's Highway. (Which was the route Moses sought to follow while leading the exodus, but was refused access by King Sihon.) Across the river is the territory allotted to the tribe of Reuben. The people of Moab had opposed Israel and God would eventually warn them that they needed to repent or face judgment, as written in the book of Isaiah: *"For it shall be, that, as a wandering bird cast out of the nest, so the daughters of Moab shall be at the fords of Arnon.* (Isaiah 16:2)

Naomi and Ruth spend the night on the soft grass beside the river, lulled to sleep by its music. At this point the river is not the raging torrent it becomes many miles downstream, where it flows through the gorge and plunges into the sea. Here it flows more calmly, singing the songs that rivers sometimes sing. At dawn, the rising sun turns the rocks of the canyon fiery red as the morning mists melt away into the glory of a new day. Naomi and Ruth awaken and resume their trek. They ford across the stream at a shallow spot as the sun rises higher in the sky. They have traveled across the plains of Moab and still have a long way to go since it is a trip of about 70 miles. This road will take Naomi back to her home town and people that she knows. It will take Ruth to a place where she will be a stranger to the people, its customs and its religion. For both of them it will prove to be a road *to tomorrow*, which will be better than the past.

The two women now turn west toward their final objective. They will have to make one more difficult crossing, the Jordan River, where it flows 825 feet below sea level through the Jordan Rift Valley, a gigantic scar in the earth that extends from Syria in the north to the Red Sea in the south. After plodding many miles across the hot, dusty plateau they descend the winding path down to the river. As they wade across one of the many fords, they gaze in awe at the rugged walls towering above the river on each side and wonder about the cataclysmic forces which created this great rift in the earth's surface.

The final climb is up a rocky slope towards Bethlehem, located in the limestone hills of Judea, 2500 feet above sea level. As Naomi and Ruth approach the town, they pass by the tomb of Rachel, the wife of Jacob, who died in childbirth. Naomi says a prayer then, as countless numbers of women have and still do to this day. The memory of Rachel persisted in the minds of the Jews in New Testament times, when Matthew wrote his account of Jesus' birth:

*Then Herod, when he saw that he was mocked of the wise men, was exceeding wroth, and sent forth, and slew all the children that were in Bethlehem, and in all the coasts thereof, from two years old and under, according to the time which he had diligently enquired of the wise men. Then was fulfilled that which was spoken by Jeremy the prophet, saying, In Rama was there a voice heard, lamentation, and weeping, and great mourning, Rachel weeping for her children, and would not be comforted, because they are not.* (Matthew 2:16-18)

Bethlehem is a small town whose inhabitants are mostly farmers and shepherds. The sleepy little village bestirs itself as the two women walk into town, leading their pack donkey behind them. This is a trip back in time for Naomi, returning after her long absence. For Ruth, the foreigner, it is all strange and different. Like any small town, the inhabitants are curious about anyone appearing on their streets for the first time. It is obvious these women have come a long way. They appear to be tired and walk with the slow tread of weariness. Their clothes are dusty and begrimed. People are looking and talking. Then, after a second look, a woman thinks she may recognize one of the "strangers" and says, *". . . Is this Naomi?"* to which, Naomi replies, *". . . Call me not Naomi, call me Mara:['bitter'] for the Almighty hath dealt very bitterly with me. I went out full, and the LORD hath brought me home again empty: why then call ye me Naomi, seeing the LORD hath testified against me, and the Almighty hath afflicted me?"* (Ruth 1:20-21) Naomi's home is gone, her husband and two sons are gone. It is understandable that she would feel bitter. But, God has brought her back to her hometown and given her Ruth for family. She will eventually realize that, in spite of her tragedy, God has not forsaken her. But she is not yet ready to understand this. The women of the village gather around her and console her as best they can. Ruth is not overlooked either, for they remember God's words to Israel when they first settled this land: *"And if a stranger sojourn with thee in your land, ye shall not vex him. But the stranger that dwelleth with you shall be unto you as one born among you, and thou shalt love him as thyself; for ye were strangers in the land of Egypt: I am the LORD your God."*(Leviticus 19:33-34)

The timing of their return was providential. It was the season of barley harvest. Barley was the first grain to ripen. The fields were golden with ripened heads of grain, bowing low with their burden. Each passing breeze sent ripples across the fields like ocean waves. A good barley harvest was an indication that the famine in Israel had truly ended. This harvest will prove to be a special blessing to both Naomi and Ruth.

In those days there were no welfare programs to provide for widows and orphans. They must find a way to provide for themselves. But, God in His mercy, had not forgotten the poor. Before the Jews reached this land, God had told them, *"And when ye reap the harvest of your land, thou shalt not wholly reap the corners of thy field, neither shalt thou gather the gleanings of thy harvest. And thou shalt not glean thy vineyard, neither shalt thou gather every grape of thy vineyard; thou shalt leave them for the poor and stranger: I am the LORD your God"*. (Leviticus 19:9-10) When Ruth learns about this provision for the poor, she decides to go and glean for food in the fields surrounding Bethlehem. She is not aware that God is at work in her life, guiding her steps. There were dozens of fields around Bethlehem, but Ruth chose a field belonging to a wealthy man named Boaz. Without realizing it, she had chosen a field belonging to a relative of her deceased husband, and this would bring about a remarkable change in her life.

Later in the day, when Boaz comes to visit his field, he sees Ruth and asks the servant in charge of the reapers who she is. The servant replies, *". . . It is the Moabitish damsel that came back with Naomi out of the country of Moab"* (Ruth 2:6b). Boaz then tells Ruth to stay in his field and not glean in other fields. Then he makes sure that she will be safe here and invites her to lunch with him. After lunch he instructs his servants, *". . . Let her glean even among the sheaves, and reproach her not: And let fall also some of the handfuls of purpose for her, and leave them, that she may glean them, and rebuke her not."* (Ruth 2:15b-16).

In the evening, Ruth returns home and relates the events of the day to her mother-in-law. Naomi is delighted when she learns whose field Ruth has been gleaning. She now realizes that God has not forgotten her, but His hand is at work in their lives. So Ruth gleans in the fields until the end of both the barley and the wheat harvest. At the end of the harvest, Naomi tells Ruth what she must do. Ruth follows her instructions and goes to the threshing floor where the grain is being winnowed.

Threshing floors were usually located on a hilltop open to the wind. The floors were hard packed earth or stone. Oxen would walk around in a circle on the stalks of grain. The pressure of their hooves would separate the grain from the husks. Then the mixture of grain and chaff would be winnowed by tossing it into the air with a fork. The wind would blow away the chaff and the heavier grain would fall to the floor. There was an interesting commandment regarding the oxen used in threshing: Deuteronomy 25:4 says, *"Thou shalt not muzzle the ox when he treadeth out the corn [i.e. grain]"* So even the oxen received compensation for their work.

During harvest time, families would camp near the threshing floor. (I have seen families in Romania camping in the fields under makeshift tents made of plastic sheeting, during growing season, to avoid making the trip from their homes each day to work in the crops.) In Israel, the men would sleep on the threshing floor at night to guard their precious grain. They would lie down on the floor with their heads toward the grain and feet pointed outward. At the end of a long tiring day, Boaz lies down on the threshing floor to sleep.

Then, under cover of darkness, Ruth arrives. Her actions may seem strange to us, but there is nothing improper in what she does as she follows Naomi's instructions. She uncovers Boaz's feet and lies down. At midnight, Boaz stirs in his sleep and then is startled awake when he realizes someone is lying at his feet. *"And he said, Who art thou? And she answered, I am Ruth thine handmaid: spread therefore thy skirt over thine handmaid; for thou art a near kinsman."* (Ruth 3:9) To spread the hem of one's garment over someone was a symbol of protection, like a mother bird spreading its wings over her young. Ruth was asking Boaz to marry her. Some commentators say that in Jewish weddings today, the groom spreads his talith, or prayer shawl, over the bride to signify that he is taking her under his protection.

According to Jewish law, when a man died his closest kin was expected to marry the widow and redeem his property, so the land would remain within the same tribe. *"If brethren dwell together, and one of them die, and have no child, the wife of the dead shall not marry without unto a stranger: her husband's brother shall go in unto her, and take her to him to wife, and perform the duty of an husband's brother unto her."* (Deuteronomy 25:5) However, there was one obstacle in the way for Ruth and Boaz. Another man was a closer relative than Boaz to Ruth's deceased husband. Boaz promises that he will deal with the situation and sends Ruth home to her mother-in-law.

True to his word, Boaz goes to the gate of the city and when the closest relative comes by, he tells him that someone needs to redeem the property which was formerly in Elimelech's family. The relative readily agrees to redeem the property, but when he discovers that Ruth is part of the deal he declines. He would have been glad to have the property, but does not want the responsibility of taking Ruth as a wife. Perhaps Boaz breathes a sigh of relief as he realizes that no obstacles remain in the way. He can act as the *kinsman redeemer* and marry Ruth.

Imagine the joy that came to Naomi when Ruth and Boaz became man and wife. Then, in the passing of time, when Ruth had a son, how her heart must have been overflowing as she realized that God had taken away the bitterness from her life.

> *And the women said unto Naomi, Blessed be the LORD, which hath not left thee this day without a kinsman, that his name may be famous in Israel. And he shall be unto thee a restorer of thy life, and a nourisher of thine old age: for thy daughter in law, which loveth thee, which is better to thee than seven sons, hath born him. And Naomi took the child, and laid it in her bosom, and became nurse unto it. And the women her neighbours gave it a name, saying, There is a son born to Naomi; and they called his name Obed: he is the father of Jesse, the father of David.* (Ruth 4:14-17)

The child, Obed would grow up and father a son, Jesse, who would become the father of David, the King. Now, if you jump over to the first chapter of the Gospel of Matthew you will find the genealogy of Jesus, who was born to be the Kinsman Redeemer of all who receive Him as Savior. There, you will find the names of Boaz and Ruth.

MILEPOSTS-

**Bitterness Brings Loneliness-** It alienates us from God and from those who care most about us. The loneliest people are those who have allowed the disappointments of life to make them bitter. Turn your frustrations over to God and allow Him to replace your resentment with the sweet spirit of forgiveness and hope. *"But they that wait upon the LORD shall renew their strength; they shall mount up with wings as eagles; they shall run, and not be weary; and they shall walk, and not faint."* (Isaiah 40:31)

**Lucky Break or Providence?** - Many of the things that happen to us are not due to luck, but result from the way God is working out His will for our lives. We should thank Him for watching over us and helping us to go in the right direction.

**Faith and Mercy Meet-** Ruth had the faith to be industrious gathering grain in the fields. Boaz showed mercy in his treatment of her, a poor foreigner. If you believe in God, show mercy and kindness to others.

**Law & Grace-** By the law Ruth had a right to glean among the corners of the field. By grace Boaz provided extra grain for her, and allowed her to even glean among the sheaves stacked in the field. God's grace provides for us far beyond the requirements of the law.

## 10

# The Road to the Inn

*"And all went to be taxed, every one into his own city."* (Luke 2:3)

Slowly a small caravan moves along the valley which forms the boundary between Galilee and Samaria. Named Jezreel, which means *God sows,* the valley, at this point, is actually a broad plain. It is a place of stunning natural beauty, the most fertile region in Palestine. Wide fields of wheat and barley spread out like a quilt. In the far distance to the north, the snow capped peak of Mount Hermon glows in the sun. Behind, rises Mount Carmel, where Elijah challenged and defeated the prophets of Baal. On the left is the rounded peak of Mount Tabor which, at 1,843 feet above sea level is the highest mountain in Lower Galilee. To the right, is the longer bulk of Mount Gilboa. The travelers have come from the village of Nazareth, which lies in a bowl shaped basin overlooking the valley and surrounded by limestone hills. They are traveling south-east toward the Jordan River.

The caravan consists of people traveling to the their ancestral homes to participate in the census. Caesar Augustus has decreed that everyone must register for a tax to be imposed by the Roman government. Among the travelers are a young couple, a builder named Joseph and his wife Mary, who are traveling south to Bethlehem. Both are descendants of the family of King David. They have joined together with others for the trip because it is not safe to travel alone. Joseph leads a donkey laden with provisions for the trip. Mary, who is expecting a child, walks along with him. When she grows tired, she may ride the donkey for awhile, but she must walk most of the time. Many in the group are friends and neighbors. Mary joins in conversation with them as they walk along together. Much of the time, though, she is deep in thought, reflecting on the strange events of the past year.

It all began when her cousin Elizabeth's husband saw an angel. Zacharias, a priest, had been ministering in the temple in Jerusalem, when the angel Gabriel appeared to him and announced that Zacharias and Elizabeth would have a child.

*And Zacharias said unto the angel, Whereby shall I know this? for I am an old man, and my wife well stricken in years. And the angel answering said unto him, I am Gabriel, that stand in the presence of God; and am sent to speak unto thee, and to shew thee these glad tidings. And, behold, thou shalt be dumb, and not able to speak, until the day that these things shall be performed, because thou believest not my words, which shall be fulfilled in their season.* (Luke 1:18-20)

*The Road to the Inn*

It had been 400 years since Israel had heard a direct word from God. Now, this strange announcement came to Zacharias. But then, six months later, an even stranger thing happened. The angel Gabriel appeared again. This time in Nazareth, to Mary, who was espoused to Joseph.

*And the angel came in unto her, and said, Hail, thou that art highly favoured, the Lord is with thee: blessed art thou among women. And when she saw him, she was troubled at his saying, and cast in her mind what manner of salutation this should be. And the angel said unto her, Fear not, Mary: for thou hast found favour with God. And, behold, thou shalt conceive in thy womb, and bring forth a son, and shalt call his name JESUS. He shall be great, and shall be called the Son of the Highest: and the Lord God shall give unto him the throne of his father David: And he shall reign over the house of Jacob for ever; and of his kingdom there shall be no end.* (Luke 1:28-33)

Mary was puzzled by this announcement, because she was a virgin. She did not understand how she could have a child, but the angel explained: *". . . The Holy Ghost shall come upon thee, and the power of the Highest shall overshadow thee: therefore also that holy thing which shall be born of thee shall be called the Son of God."* (Luke 1:35b). Though she knew that this would make life difficult for her because others would not know nor believe the circumstances, Mary willingly submitted to the will of God.

Immediately after this announcement, Mary traveled south from Galilee to the hill country of Judea, near Hebron, for a three month visit with her cousin Elizabeth. When she arrived, another strange thing happened. Elizabeth's baby leaped in her womb, *"And she spake out with a loud voice, and said, Blessed art thou among women, and blessed is the fruit of thy womb. And whence is this to me, that the mother of my Lord should come to me?"* (Luke 1:42-43). Elizabeth's son, John, the Baptist, would be the forerunner, or herald, of Jesus. He would prepare people for the beginning of Jesus' ministry. Some have referred to this as John's first prophecy regarding Jesus.

As the caravan moved across the valley of Jezreel, it paused at the town of Beth Shean, where more travelers joined the group for the trip south. The valley now narrowed and began its descent toward the Jordan River. The landscape changed from flat and green to steep and rugged. Mary's thoughts turned to the events of the previous months and how these things would affect her and her family. Their lives would be changed in ways she could not foresee and she prayed for strength to bear it all. She knew that the baby she carried was from God and that He would have an impact on history far beyond anyone else who had ever lived. It was almost too much to be contained.

When they reached the bottom of the steep descent, they came to one of the fords across the river, there were no bridges. Wading across the river, they turned southward. The would stay on the east side of

## The Road to the Inn

the Jordan because the Jews and Samaritans did not get along, so it was best to avoid the west bank which ran through Samaria. They traveled down the Jordan Valley, a deep rift in the earth's surface. It was hotter here than in the upland valley. They followed the general course of the river, but not every bend, which would have lengthened the distance considerably.

As they walked southward, Joseph turned over in his mind the things that had recently happened to him. While he and Mary had been engaged, it became apparent that she was expecting a child and Joseph did not know the circumstances of the conception. Since an engagement was as binding as a marriage, the normal thing to do was to divorce her and send her away. Joseph loved Mary and did not want to subject her to public shame, so he thought about putting her away privately, to spare her embarrassment. Then, one night, he had a vivid dream:

*But while he thought on these things, behold, the angel of the Lord appeared unto him in a dream, saying, Joseph, thou son of David, fear not to take unto thee Mary thy wife: for that which is conceived in her is of the Holy Ghost. And she shall bring forth a son, and thou shalt call his name JESUS: for he shall save his people from their sins. Now all this was done, that it might be fulfilled which was spoken of the Lord by the prophet, saying, Behold, a virgin shall be with child, and shall bring forth a son, and they shall call his name Emmanuel, which being interpreted is, God with us. Then Joseph being raised from sleep did as the angel of the Lord had bidden him, and took unto him his wife:* (Matthew 1:20-24)

Now, because of what God had revealed to him in the dream, Joseph understood that Mary had not been unfaithful to him. God had, through His miraculous power, caused a child to be conceived within her. She was still a virgin, but she would be the mother of God's Son, Jesus. As they continued their journey, both Joseph and Mary turned all these things over in their minds and wondered about how this would affect their future.

The caravan continued down the Jordan Valley until they came to the place where they would again ford across the river. They waded across and came to the city of Jericho, which was located at an oasis. Jericho was known as "The City of Palms" because of all the palm trees that grew there, and it brought a welcome respite for the weary travelers. After resting there awhile, they began the long, steep climb up toward Bethlehem. They had been traveling for a week and looked forward to arriving at their destination.

As they approached Bethlehem, they passed by the tomb of Rachel, who had died in childbirth. Mary was sad as she thought about that, but then she remembered that long ago, Ruth had also come this way with Naomi, who was returning from Moab. Ruth found a new life and a new husband in Bethlehem. She had become the mother of the lineage of David the king, from whom both Mary and Joseph were descended.

## The Road to the Inn

Arriving at Bethlehem, the caravan ended its journey at a caravansary, or inn. The inn consisted of two stories. The upper story contained rooms for travelers and the lower story was made up of stalls for animals, around an open courtyard. The rooms were all taken, so Mary and Joseph stayed on the ground floor. It was not unusual, in that day, for people and animals to occupy the same living quarters. Soon, birth pangs began and Mary went into labor.

*And so it was, that, while they were there, the days were accomplished that she should be delivered. And she brought forth her firstborn son, and wrapped him in swaddling clothes, and laid him in a manger; because there was no room for them in the inn.* (Luke 2:6-7)

On a hillside, about a mile outside Bethlehem, near the road from Jerusalem, stands the Tower of Migdal Eder. The tower was used by shepherds to watch for wild animals or marauding bands of thieves that would decimate their flocks. The sheep that were kept here were destined to become sacrificial lambs. The tower was also used as a birthplace for lambs. When they were born, they were wrapped in swaddling clothes and laid in a manger to protect them because they would be offered as a sacrifice in the Temple at Jerusalem. Many years ago, the prophet Micah had prophesied, *"And thou, O tower of the flock, the strong hold of the daughter of Zion, unto thee shall it come, even the first dominion; the kingdom shall come to the daughter of Jerusalem."* (Micah 4:8). On this night, as the shepherds kept their lonely watch, they were startled when a bright light turned the night into day and an angel appeared:

> *And there were in the same country shepherds abiding in the field, keeping watch over their flock by night. And, lo, the angel of the Lord came upon them, and the glory of the Lord shone round about them: and they were sore afraid. And the angel said unto them, Fear not: for, behold, I bring you good tidings of great joy, which shall be to all people. For unto you is born this day in the city of David a Saviour, which is Christ the Lord. And this shall be a sign unto you; Ye shall find the babe wrapped in swaddling clothes, lying in a manger. And suddenly there was with the angel a multitude of the heavenly host praising God, and saying, Glory to God in the highest, and on earth peace, good will toward men.* (Luke 2:8-14)

Then, as quickly as they had appeared, the angels vanished from their sight. Immediately, the shepherds left their herds and rushed to Bethlehem, where they found Mary and Joseph, with a newborn baby, lying in a manger. After seeing the child, the shepherds did not hesitate, but told everyone they saw about the visitation of angels and what they had seen in Bethlehem.

Mary never forgot this night, *"But Mary kept all these things, and pondered them in her heart."* (Luke 2:19). God had chosen a simple virgin from the hill country of Nazareth to bear His Only Begotten Son in the little town of Bethlehem. The announcement of

His birth was not made to kings or the upper class, but to shepherds, a class of people who were looked down upon by society. When Jesus grew to manhood and began to preach, He would say, *"...Blessed be ye poor: for yours is the kingdom of God."* (Luke 6:20). The majority of those who would listen and follow Him would be the poor, the downtrodden, the outcast and rejected members of society. He made God's grace available to both the rich and the poor, the educated and uneducated, the upstanding and the downcast. He was God's love made visible in human flesh.

MILEPOSTS-

**The Hinge of History** - The birth of Jesus in Bethlehem was so important that the calendar was altered to reflect two eras in human history. Years before His birth are labeled **BC** (Before Christ) and the years after His birth are labeled **AD** (Anno Domini, The Year of Our Lord).

**Why Was He Born?** - From the days of Adam and Eve, mankind has existed in a lost estate, separated by sin from God the Father. But God did not leave us to our fate. Because He loves us, He sent His Son into the world, to live, to die for our sins, and to rise again, so that we could saved from our lost condition and know the joy of living in fellowship with Him in this world and be blessed with eternal life in Heaven.

**How He Was Received** - One would think that the entire world would rejoice and receive Him, but not so. When Jesus was born, Herod tried to kill Him. During

His ministry, He was opposed by the very people to whom He had come: *"He came unto his own, and his own received him not."* (John 1:11). But others have received Him, down through the ages since: *". . . as many as received him, to them gave he power to become the sons of God, even to them that believe on his name"* (John 1:12)

## 11

# The Road to the Star

*"I shall see him, but not now: I shall behold him, but not nigh: there shall come a Star out of Jacob, and a Sceptre shall rise out of Israel..."* (Numbers 24:17a)

The ear-numbing roar subsides as the wind diminishes from a gale to a gentle breeze. Impenetrable darkness gives way to a brown haze, which gradually clears, leaving a blue sky and bright sunlight. On the ground numerous piles of sand stir and begin to rise. They shake and the sand falls away, revealing that the larger lumps are camels and the smaller ones are men, who had sheltered next to them.

Several hours ago, a wall of sand was spotted, moving with incredible speed directly toward the caravan. Quickly, the camels were forced to lie down on the ground and, wrapping themselves tightly in their robes, the men lay down beside them. Swallowed up by the swirling sandstorm, there was nothing more that could be done, and the members of the desert caravan were forced to lie helpless as the cloud of sand turned day into night. The shrieking wind blasted everything with stinging, smothering grains of sand. Their only hope had been that the sandstorm would move on before suffocating men and beasts.

Once the sandstorm passed on, camel drivers checked the lashings on the camel's burdens and began to line them up, fastening each one behind another. By traveling in single file the first camels in line would make a deep track through the sand for those that followed. The journey would continue through sand and across hard packed, arid ground.

There are hundreds of men, and camels in this caravan, including servants and a large number of soldiers who provide protection from the bandits and robbers who commonly prey on travelers. The rest of the contingent are powerful king makers, the Magi (Hebrew *rab-mag*) from the ancient land of the Babylonian Empire, which was followed by the Medo-Persian Empire. Without their support, no one could become king in the land of the Medes and Persians. They were making this journey, following a star, which they had seen in the East, to find the child who had been born "King of the Jews". For many years there had been a tradition in the Orient that one would come from Judea who would rule the world, and these men were familiar with this tradition, as well as the history and prophecies of the Jews.

In 605 BC Nebuchadnezzar had conquered Judah and taken the Jews as captives to the land of Babylon. *"By the rivers of Babylon, there we sat down, yea, we wept, when we remembered Zion. We hanged our harps upon the willows in the midst thereof. For there they that carried us away captive required of us a song; and they that wasted us required of us mirth, saying, Sing us one of the songs of Zion. How shall we sing the LORD'S song in a strange land?"* (Psalm 137:1-4)

Among those captives was a teenager named Daniel. Because Daniel was able to interpret a dream that Nebuchadnezzar had, when all the wise men had failed, he was made a master over the wise men of Babylon: *"Then the king made Daniel a great man, and gave him many great gifts, and made him ruler over the whole province of Babylon, and chief of the governors over all the **wise men** of Babylon."* (Daniel 2:48).

Later, the Jews were allowed to return home. Some went, but many continued to live in Babylon. So, the Magi, or wise men, were familiar with the history of Daniel and his prophecies regarding the succession of kingdoms from Babylonian, to Medo-Persian, to Greek, and the Roman Empire of their day. They probably knew about Balaam's prophecy, as well, *"I shall see him, but not now: I shall behold him, but not nigh: there shall come a **Star** out of Jacob, and a Sceptre shall rise out of Israel. . . "* (Numbers 24:17a). So, the Magi who were students of astrology and astronomy, were continually watching the night sky. When a new star appeared, these men knew it signified an important event, so they began preparations for a long journey to find the King of the Jews.

The trek was a long and arduous one, which involved walking nearly a thousand miles over difficult terrain which included sand, rock and lava flow. The sun beat down upon them relentlessly during the day and the nights were extremely cold. Water was available only at the occasional oasis. Camels can go five days without water in the heat of the desert, averaging two to three miles per hour for eight to fifteen hours. The caravan traveled during the day, except when the heat was excessive. When the heat became unbearable they would rest during the day and travel at night. All their food and water had to be carried with them and the men slept on the ground whenever there was a stop for rest.

Eventually, this group reached the land of the Nabateans, an ancient and once powerful people who became wealthy by developing caravan routes through the desert. Water was available from cisterns which collected dew that settled on the rocks at night. The Nabatean city of Petra was lost for centuries until it was rediscovered by archaeologists in the 1800's. It was a magnificent city carved in the cliffs and rose colored rocks, located in the middle of Jordan's desert. Today, tourists go there and marvel at the engineering wonders of the people who did such difficult, and beautiful work.

Upon reaching the land of the Nabateans, the Magi's caravan followed the King's Highway, which ran north and south. Then turning west again they descended to the Jordan River, crossing it near Jericho, at an altitude of 1200 feet **below** sea level. From there they had a steep climb up to Jerusalem, situated at 2550 feet **above** sea level. It was, naturally, assumed that a king born to the Jews would be found in Jerusalem, but, when the wise men asked, *"Saying, Where is he that is born King of the Jews? for we have seen his star in the east, and are come to worship him."* (Matthew 2:2), no one seemed to know. This was a politically loaded question, however, and word soon reached Herod that men, accompanied by their own army, were looking for a rival king. It just happened that, at the time, Herod's army was away fighting another battle. So it is no wonder that he was extremely upset.

> *When Herod the king had heard these things, he was troubled, and all Jerusalem with him. And when he had gathered all the chief priests and scribes of the people together, he demanded of them where Christ should be born. And they said unto him, In Bethlehem of Judaea: for thus it is written by the prophet, And thou Bethlehem, in the land of Juda, art not the least among the princes of Juda: for out of thee shall come a Governor, that shall rule my people Israel. Then Herod, when he had privily called the wise men, enquired of them diligently what time the star appeared. And he sent them to Bethlehem, and said, Go and search diligently for the young child; and when ye have found him, bring me word again, that I may come and worship him also.*
> (Matthew 2:3-8)

Of course, Herod had no intention of worshipping the child. He merely wanted to find out where his rival to the throne was located, so he could eliminate him. The Magi, though, had endured the hardships of a long and difficult journey because they really did desire to worship the young child. The star which they had followed on their journey, was now standing over Bethlehem. *"When they had heard the king, they departed; and, lo, the star, which they saw in the east, went before them, till it came and stood over where the young child was. When they saw the star, they rejoiced with exceeding great joy."* (Matthew 2:9-10) Thus, the journey was continued to Bethlehem, the place where Ruth had lived, after she married Boaz, and the town that King David called home.

Pastor-Teacher John MacArthur describes Bethlehem this way: "Bethlehem is a quiet little town, approximately five or six miles south of Jerusalem. It was once called "Ephrathah," and was so designated by the Old Testament prophet Micah. The name Bethlehem actually means "house of bread" (Hebrew: beth = "house"; lehem = "bread"). It was a fitting name for the place where the very Bread of Life was born (see John 6:48). Sitting in a fertile countryside about twenty-five hundred feet high in altitude, this little village was very productive. It is saddled on a ridge between two higher summits, which makes it look as though it is set in an amphitheater. And because its buildings are for the most part constructed out of the gray limestone on which the town rests, it appears as if the buildings simply rise up out of the ground."

When the Magi arrived, it was some time after the birth of Jesus. He was no longer a baby, but a young child, living in a house, not a stable. They bowed in worhip before Him and presented Him gifts of gold, frankincense, and myrrh. *"And when they were come into the house, they saw the young child with Mary his mother, and fell down, and worshipped him: and when they had opened their treasures, they presented unto him gifts; gold, and frankincense, and myrrh."*

(Matthew 2:11) Frankincense was used in worship and it was obtained from the sap of a tree that grows on the edge of the desert. Myrrh came from a tree resembling acacia. It was one of the ingredients in holy anointing oil and was used as a perfume and in embalming.

What was the star the Magi followed? There have been many theories about it, but if you think back to the time of the Exodus, you will remember that the Israelites were led by a cloud by day and a glowing fire by night. This shining light was the Shekinah glory of God. Jesus' birth was announced to shepherds by an angel, accompanied by the bright, visible glory of the presence of God: *"And, lo, the angel of the Lord came upon them, and the glory of the Lord shone round about them: and they were sore afraid."* (Luke 2:9). The star then, must have been this same shining glory. It was the glory of God that led the Magis to Bethlehem, where they became the first Gentiles to worship the Son of God. Remember, when God called Abraham, He promised to bless him, his descendants and ultimately all the nations through him. *"Now the Scripture foresaw that God would justify the Gentiles by faith and foretold the good news to Abraham, saying, All the nations will be blessed in you."* (Galatians 3:8 HCSB) This promise was fulfilled with the birth of Jesus.

A friend, Dr. D. B. Martin of Virginia Beach, Virginia was in Israel recently and spent one day in Bethlehem and Hebron. He relates the following, "While we were at the Church of the Nativity in Bethlehem, our Arabic guide told us an interesting story. He said that when the Muslims took over Jerusalem, Bethlehem and what we call Holy

Land, that all the churches built largely by Emperor Constantine's mother, in the Holy land were destroyed except the Church of the Nativity in Bethlehem. He went on to say that there was a large painting of the wisemen, which appeared to be very authentic, i.e. the men looked like and were dressed like men from the East. The Muslim leaders were impressed with the painting of the wise men and thought if wisemen from the east came there that made it a holy place and they did not destroy that church. I had never heard that before but found it very interesting. This Arabic guide was born in Bethlehem and had lived there all his life."

Having worshipped Jesus and given him gifts, the Magi did not return to Jerusalem and Herod, but went home by a different route: *"And being warned of God in a dream that they should not return to Herod, they departed into their own country another way."* (Matthew 2:12)

Meanwhile, Herod, having ascertained the approximate time of Jesus' birth goes about his plans to annihilate any rival to his position: *"Then Herod, when he saw that he was mocked of the wise men, was exceeding wroth, and sent forth, and slew all the children that were in Bethlehem, and in all the coasts thereof, from two years old and under, according to the time which he had diligently enquired of the wise men."* (Matthew 2:16)

Herod was of mixed lineage, half Jew and half Idumaean, being a partial descendant of the Edomites who lived southeast of Israel and who were traditionally enemies of the Jews. He was king only because the Romans had no regard for the religion or traditions of the people they conquered. Herod also was an extremely cruel man. He killed his own wife, Mariamne and her mother, Alexandra. He ordered the execution of two of his sons, and just before his death, he had another son killed. Is it any wonder that he ordered the slaying of innocent children to protect his throne?

But Herod did not succeed in getting rid of the child whose star the Wise Men had followed to Bethlehem: *"And when they were departed, behold, the angel of the Lord appeareth to Joseph in a dream, saying, Arise, and take the young child and his mother, and flee into Egypt, and be thou there until I bring thee word: for Herod will seek the young child to destroy him. When he arose, he took the young child and his mother by night, and departed into Egypt: And was there until the death of Herod: that it might be fulfilled which was spoken of the Lord by the prophet, saying, Out of Egypt have I called my son."* (Matthew 2:13-15). The gold that the Magi had given to the child was probably a great help during their stay in Egypt.

After the death of Herod, Joseph brought his family back to Israel, settling in the city of Nazareth. *"And he came and dwelt in a city called Nazareth: that it might be fulfilled which was spoken by the prophets, He shall be called a Nazarene. "* (Matthew 2:23). During His ministry, Jesus was often referred to as having come from Nazareth. The Bible makes it clear that He first came from Heaven to earth as God's greatest love gift to mankind.

MILEPOSTS-

**Going home a different way-** The Bible tells us the Magi went home *"another way"*. It could well be said that everyone who has ever met Jesus and truly worshipped Him, will go home a different person than when they came. What difference has He made in your life?

**The death of the innocents-** It is heartbreaking to think of the innocent children slain by Herod in his lust for power. We tend to think of that as something possible only in ancient history, but what about the innocent children killed by abortion? There are those today who have as little regard for the sanctity of human life as Herod.

**A dangerous place for the Son of God-** Jesus birth was announced by angels. He was worshipped by shepherds and wise men. Common people adored Him. But, the powerful of the world were always plotting to kill Him. Persecution rained down upon His followers. Today, things have not changed much. There are those who worship Him and there are those who attack Him by attacking believers.

**Jesus will return for His own-** He will come first for His Bride, the church (i.e. all who have trusted in Him as their Savior). This has been referred to as the "Rapture" which is described in 1 Thessalonians 4:16-17, *"For the Lord himself shall descend from heaven with a shout, with the voice of the archangel, and with the trump of God: and the dead in Christ shall rise first: Then we which are alive and remain shall be caught up together with them in the clouds, to meet the Lord in the air: and so shall we ever be with the Lord."* Are you ready, or will you be left behind?

**The coming of the King-** The first time Jesus came to earth, he was born in a manger. This same Jesus is coming again as King. Following the Rapture, the earth will go through the worst time in its history, referred to as the "Great Tribulation". Jesus, Himself, tells us what will happen, in Matthew 24:29-30, *"Immediately after the tribulation of those days shall the sun be darkened, and the moon shall not give her light, and the stars shall fall from heaven, and the powers of the heavens shall be shaken: And then shall appear the sign of the Son of man in heaven: and then shall all the tribes of the earth mourn, and they shall see the Son of man coming in the clouds of heaven with power and great glory."* Judgment Day is coming. Are you ready?

**Which star are you following?** - In past ages people fawned over royalty and the nobility. Today, many are fascinated by the stars of Hollywood, music, or sports. Remember, the Star of the Bible, from Genesis to Revelation is Jesus.

## 12

# The King's Highway

*"The voice of him that crieth in the wilderness, Prepare ye the way of the LORD, make straight in the desert a highway for our God."* (Isaiah 40:3)

The common people of Judea were flocking in droves to a rugged and remote area on the Jordan river near Jericho. They were coming to see a strange man, who lived like a hermit in the wilderness. The crowds curiosity had been aroused because it was rumored that a prophet had appeared. It had been four hundred years since Israel had heard from a prophet of God, so they were eager to see and hear the one who was preaching and baptizing people in the Jordan. As they were talking and speculating about just what it all might mean, out of desert strode a wild looking man with long hair and a beard. It was John, the son of Zacharias, a priest who lived in the hill country of Judea. John wore clothing made of camels hair, a leather belt, and lived off of wild locusts and honey. Now, some have questioned the meaning of the word *locusts* and have interpreted it to mean the fruit of a locust tree. But in the Old

Testament, the Jews had been given permission to eat certain insects, *"Even these of them ye may eat; the locust after his kind, and the bald locust after his kind, and the beetle after his kind, and the grasshopper after his kind."* (Leviticus 11:22). Locusts were sun dried or roasted and are rumored to taste like shrimp. (While in South America, I had the opportunity to sample roasted termites. They tasted like burnt paper to me, but it is rumored that some insects are quite tasty and nutritious.)

Thirty years before, an angel had appeared to Zacharias, as he ministered in the temple at Jerusalem. The angel told him that he and his wife, Elisabeth, would have a son and his name should be called John. Zacharias and Elisabeth were well advanced in age, and he questioned how a couple as old as they could have a son. For this he was stricken mute and was unable to speak until their son was born. The angel said that John would be filled with the Holy Spirit, and prepare the people for the coming of the Messiah. *"For he shall be great in the sight of the Lord, and shall drink neither wine nor strong drink; and he shall be filled with the Holy Ghost, even from his mother's womb. And many of the children of Israel shall he turn to the Lord their God."* (Luke 1:15-16)

Now, John at the age of thirty, was living in the wilderness and preaching to the multitudes who came out to hear him. His mission was to prepare the way for the coming of the Messiah.

*And he came into all the country about Jordan, preaching the baptism of repentance for the remission of sins; As it is written in*

*the book of the words of Esaias the prophet, saying, The voice of one crying in the wilderness, Prepare ye the way of the Lord, make his paths straight. Every valley shall be filled, and every mountain and hill shall be brought low; and the crooked shall be made straight, and the rough ways shall be made smooth; And all flesh shall see the salvation of God.*
(Luke 3:3-6)

In those days, when a king planned to tour his realm he would send out workers to prepare the roads he would be traveling. They would work on the roads leveling out the high places, filling in the low spots and straightening the road as much as possible. Stones and other obstacles in the road were removed to make the passage of the king's chariot easier. The obstacles that John dealt with were not physical, but spiritual. The greatest obstacle consisted of the sins of the people. Like their ancestors they had drifted away from God. They were not living in anticipation of the Messiah's advent. They were unaware that He had been born in Bethlehem about thirty years before and was soon to appear on the scene. John did not preach an easy believism, but demanded proof of genuine heart felt repentance. Repenting of sin would remove the obstructions on the road into their hearts.

*Bring forth therefore fruits meet for repentance: And think not to say within yourselves, We have Abraham to our father: for I say unto you, that God is able of these stones to raise up children unto Abraham. And now also the axe is laid unto the root of the trees: therefore every tree which bringeth not forth good fruit is hewn down, and cast into the fire. I indeed baptize you with water unto repentance: but he that cometh after me is mightier than I, whose shoes I am not worthy to bear: he shall baptize you with the Holy Ghost, and with fire:* (Matthew 3:8-11)

Multitudes heard and accepted the message of John. They came from all over the land to be baptized of him in the Jordan and prepare themselves for the coming of the Messiah. Then one day Jesus appeared at the Jordan and asked John to baptize Him. John, at first declined, saying he was not worthy and that he needed to be baptized by Jesus. But Jesus insisted, so John baptized Him. *"After Jesus was baptized, He went up immediately from the water. The heavens suddenly opened for Him, and He saw the Spirit of God descending like a dove and coming down on Him. And there came a voice from heaven: This is My beloved Son. I take delight in Him!"* (Matthew 3:13-17 HCSB)

John continued his fearless preaching of the truth in the wilderness, until word reached King Herod that John had said it was not lawful for him to have his brother's wife, Herodias. Then Herod had John arrested and thrown into prison. On Herod's birthday, he gave a great party. The daughter of Herodias danced before Herod and he was so pleased that he promised her whatever she wanted. When she asked her mother what she should request, her mother saw an opportunity for revenge and told her to ask for the head of John the Baptist. Herod had John beheaded and his head was presented to Herodias on a platter. John had been faithful unto death. He preached the message he had been given fearlessly and to everyone who came to hear him, without favor or prejudice. Jesus once said of him, *"Verily I say unto you, Among them that are born of women there hath not risen a greater than John the Baptist: notwithstanding he that is least in the kingdom of heaven is greater than he."* (Matthew 11:11). What a wonderful thing, to be praised by the Savior. Then, sometime after John's death, Jesus said of him, *"He was a burning and a shining light: and ye were willing for a season to rejoice in his light."* (John 5:35)

MILEPOSTS-

**The road into your heart-** What are the obstacles on the road into your heart that prevent the entrance of the Messiah? Do you need to repent and invite Jesus into your heart? The word *repent* is translated from the Greek word *metanoeo* and means to change your mental attitude and behavior. It is a change of direction from going away from God to going His way. It means changing from being indifferent to Him to loving Him with all your heart. When someone repents he stops loving sin and begins to hate it, he finds a new love for God and a life worth living.

**Don't fear rejection-** It makes no difference who you are, or what you have done; when you turn to God in repentance and ask His forgiveness, He will forgive you. That is why Jesus came to earth, to remove the sin that separates us from God. He loves you and died on the cross so we can be forgiven and enjoy a life in fellowship with God, both here and in the hereafter.

**Worth it all-** John the Baptist risked everything in preaching the truth. He was filled with the Holy Spirit and fearlessly fulfilled his purpose in life, which was to prepare the way for the Messiah (Jesus). He gave his life in service to God. It is worth whatever risk we take to faithfully live for, and serve the Lord. Heaven is the reward.

## 13

# The Road to Everywhere

*". . . and he saith unto him, Follow me. And he arose, and followed him".* (Matthew 9:9)

The raucous cries of seagulls shattered the tranquility of early morning, as they cart wheeled and dipped over the boats. Fishermen were returning from an all night fishing foray on the waters of Galilee. Approaching the shore, they ran their boats up on the beach and dropped the sails. Jumping out of the boats into ankle deep water, they began to unload the fish. By the time they had finished unloading, the local tax collector, Levi, appeared on the shore. It was his duty to tally the catch and collect taxes on every fish brought ashore. When he had finished, he walked back to his customs and tax booth, located between the shore and the city of Capernaum.

Capernaum, a prosperous fishing port on the northwestern shore of the sea of Galilee, was a city of thirty thousand inhabitants. Located at the crossroads of international trade routes, it was a center of political and commercial business, including a Roman military post and an important tax and customs office. Roman roads were built with a foundation

## The Road to Everywhere

of stone and surfaced with large thick stones. Some were up to three feet thick, and can still be used today. The most important roads in Palestine passed by Capernaum. Roman soldiers patrolled these roads to protect those who used them from roving bandits. The Kings Highway came by there from the Red Sea. The Via Maris or *Way of the Sea*, ran up from Egypt along the shores of the Mediterranean. The Spice Road came from places as far away as India. All these connected with the crossroads by Capernaum, known as the *Road to Everywhere*.

Levi, son of Alphaeus, was a tax collector who probably worked for a Publican, such as Zaccheus (the short man who climbed a tree in order to see Jesus). Publicans contracted with the despised Roman government. They were allowed to collect whatever amount they desired, as long as they sent the correct total to Rome. Publicans and tax collectors were hated by the Jews and classified as being among the worst of sinners. They were not allowed to testify in Jewish courts and a Jew would not even accept change from a tax collector, considering it "unclean".

Just as today, there were numerous taxes to be paid. There were poll taxes, income taxes, real estate taxes and taxes on farm produce. Import and export duties were collected on the public highways and at sea ports. Travelers on major highways were charged toll fees for the maintenance of roads. There were so many taxes that they imposed a great burden on the people, making it difficult for them to survive.

At his tax office, near the road which led by the shore, Levi was in an ideal place to observe all who passed by and make sure they paid taxes on the business they conducted. Mesopotamians, Egyptians, Arabians, Indians, Turks and businessmen from Rome, all had to deal with him. Caravans of camels and donkeys from the exotic East passed by his booth, carrying silks, perfumes, baskets, pottery, and objects made of wood, silver, and brass. When caravans from the far corners of the earth arrived at Capernaum they would be compelled to unload and unpack their bundles, submit to inventory, and pay tax on their wares. Fishermen were required to pay taxes on the fish they caught and exported. Farmers paid taxes on the wheat that was grown in the area. Individuals were constantly coming by to pay the taxes assessed on them. Tax collectors like Levi became wealthy men by collecting more than required and keeping the surplus for themselves. There was a different kind of life in Levi's future, however, for one day he would meet Jesus.

Jesus was born in Bethlehem but grew up in Nazareth. He was referred to, at that time, as a Nazarene. When He began His ministry, He moved to Capernaum, as described in Matthew 4:13-16:

*And leaving Nazareth, he came and dwelt in Capernaum, which is upon the sea coast, in the borders of Zabulon and Nephthalim: That it might be fulfilled which was spoken by Esaias the prophet, saying, The land of Zabulon, and the land of Nephthalim, by the way of the sea, beyond Jordan, Galilee of the Gentiles; The people which sat in darkness saw great light; and to them which sat in the region and shadow of death light is sprung up.*

It was at Capernaum that Jesus called the first Apostles, two sets of brothers:

*Now as he walked by the sea of Galilee, he saw Simon and Andrew his brother casting a net into the sea: for they were fishers. And Jesus said unto them, Come ye after me, and I will make you to become fishers of men. And straightway they forsook their nets, and followed him. And when he had gone a little further thence, he saw James the son of Zebedee, and John his brother, who also were in the ship mending their nets. And straightway he called them: and they left their father Zebedee in the ship with the hired servants, and went after him. And they went into Capernaum; and straightway on the sabbath day he entered into the synagogue, and taught. And they were astonished at his doctrine: for he taught them as one that had authority, and not as the scribes.* (Mark 1:16-22)

The synagogue at Capernaum had been built, not by a Jew, but by a Roman Centurion. This was the same Centurion, whose servant Jesus would heal when requested to do so by the elders of the Jews, *"And when they came to Jesus, they besought him instantly, saying, That he was worthy for whom he should do this: For he loveth our nation, and he hath built us a synagogue."* (Luke 7:1-5). The ruins of this synagogue have been excavated by archaeologists and are seen today by visitors to the Holy Land.

One day, as Levi was busy haggling with people over their taxes something happened that changed his life for time and eternity: Jesus walked by and stopped at his table, *"And after these things he went forth, and saw a publican, named Levi, sitting at the receipt of custom: and he said unto him, Follow me. And he left all, rose up, and followed him."* (Luke 5:27-28)

As Jesus spoke, Levi was astonished that he should be chosen to follow Him. He had seen Jesus before as He moved about Capernaum. Though he was excluded from the synagogue, because he was a tax collector, Levi listened as Jesus spoke on the streets and by the seaside. The things He said carried the weight of authority. He spoke as One who knew what He was talking about, not like other teachers, who just repeated what they learned from a book. Jesus had done many miracles that were seen by thousands of people and Levi had witnessed some of them. Also, he was aware that Jesus had called Andrew, Peter, James and John to follow him. Perhaps he had even talked with Jesus, before this. But he had never thought that Jesus would call someone like him. Levi's heart leaped in his chest as it sank in that he was being chosen and called to follow Jesus and be one of his Apostles. He did not hesitate for a minute, but rose up out of his seat and left the tax booth. Levi gave his whole heart and life to Jesus. He immediately began to share the good news with his friends: people who were outcasts, people who needed forgiveness for their sins, people who needed a new beginning in life.

> *And Levi made him a great feast in his own house: and there was a great company of publicans and of others that sat down with them. But their scribes and Pharisees murmured against his disciples, saying, Why do ye eat and drink with publicans and sinners? And Jesus answering said unto them, They that are whole need not a physician; but they that are sick. I came not to call the righteous, but sinners to repentance.* (Luke 5:29-32)

Levi was given a new life and a new name, Matthew, which means *Gift of God*. He would write the book we call "The Gospel according to Matthew". Matthew's Gospel is known for its emphasis on Jesus' teaching. It has been referred to as the *Gospel of the Church*, since it is the only one of the four that uses the word church. It emphasizes that Christianity is the fulfillment of the Old Testament. And, it is the *Gospel of the King*, tracing the genealogy of Jesus back to David and presenting Jesus as the King Who was born in Bethlehem, was crucified on the cross, and Who will reign forever.

MILEPOSTS-

**Little is much, when God is in it -** Jesus did not choose the elite to be His Apostles. He chose common, plain fishermen and outcasts, like Levi to receive His training and carry the Gospel to the world. He delights in taking ordinary people and transforming them into heroes of the faith.

**Jesus is Who you need** - Levi needed more than a teacher. He needed more than a good example. He needed more than rules and regulations. What he needed was a Savior who would redeem his life and forgive his sins. Everyone needs to be rescued from the mess they have made of their life. Jesus rescues, redeems and gives a new life to anyone who will believe on Him and commit their life to Him.

**Don't waste your blessings** - The city of Capernaum was the home of Andrew, Peter, James, John and Matthew. Jesus made it His home and the center of His ministry. It was a place from which the Gospel could easily be carried to the world. The city was exalted by its opportunities. Yet, the population, as a whole did not repent of their sins and receive Jesus. What should have been a great blessing, became a curse, as recorded in Matthew 11:23-24 *"And thou, Capernaum, which art exalted unto heaven, shalt be brought down to hell: for if the mighty works, which have been done in thee, had been done in Sodom, it would have remained until this day. But I say unto you, That it shall be more tolerable for the land of Sodom in the day of judgment, than for thee."* Someday, we will all give an account to God for the blessings and opportunities He has given us and how we have used or misused them. Redeem the time, for the days are evil.

## 14

# Alone Beside the Highway

*"Then the eyes of the blind shall be opened, and the ears of the deaf shall be unstopped."* (Isaiah 35:5)

There were two cities named Jericho, both located in the Judean desert four miles from the Jordan river on a plain that was 800 feet below sea level. The old city had been destroyed by Joshua and lay in ruins. About a mile south, the new Jericho had been built by the Romans in an oasis, watered by streams from the mountains. It had many fine buildings including the winter palace of Herod the Great. A well traveled road came from the ford of the Jordan river, passed by both the old and the new Jericho and continued to Jerusalem, 15 miles away. Travelers following this road faced a steep climb to Jerusalem, which was 3,000 feet higher than Jericho.

Beside the road sat a man dressed in rags, begging. He had no other way to earn a living because he was blind, an affliction shared by many in the Middle East. One out of every five people had some form of eye disease, aggravated by the fine dust the breeze carried everywhere. Bartimaeus lived in a world of darkness.

He had never seen a blue sky, flowers, trees, or mountains. He had never marveled at a sunrise or watched the light play upon water. All the wonderful colors and shadings in nature meant nothing to him. He could feel the hot sun and the movement of the wind. He could hear others speaking, as they walked along the road. But he had never looked upon their faces.

Passover season was drawing near and people were passing by all the time on their way to and from Jerusalem. Some saw him and dropped a few coins in his cup, which was music to his ears. Most ignored him, focused on their own business. As Bartimaeus heard the footsteps of the passing crowd, he hoped that the increased traffic would bring more money for his needs. Occasionally, a passing acquaintance or a family member would stop and talk with him for awhile, easing the loneliness of his dark existence. As he sat listening to the conversations of people going by, he became aware that the noise had increased. The road was obviously packed with people and he could feel that they were crowding ever closer to him. Someone important must be approaching.

Among the crowd of pilgrims on their way to Jerusalem to celebrate the Passover, were Jesus and His disciples. After spending some time in Galilee, they had joined with the throng traveling southward on the east side of the Jordan river. Coming through Perea, they descended to the river and forded across. Passing by the ruins of the old Jericho they came to the new Jericho, built by the Romans. As always, Jesus was surrounded by a noisy crowd of people, all jostling to get close to Him. Some were discussing the things He taught. Others recounted the miracles they had seen. Some believed, some doubted. During the journey, Jesus had told His disciples:

> *. . . Behold, we go up to Jerusalem; and the Son of man shall be delivered unto the chief priests, and unto the scribes; and they shall condemn him to death, and shall deliver him to the Gentiles: And they shall mock him, and shall scourge him, and shall spit upon him, and shall kill him: and the third day he shall rise again.* (Mark 10:33-34)

He had told them twice before that He would suffer and die, and rise again, but it just didn't seem to register with the disciples until after the resurrection, when they remembered all that He had told them. Like most Jews, they were familiar with the prophecies in the Old Testament which foretold the coming of the Messiah, who would save His people. But they had overlooked the passages about the *Suffering Servant* because they just could not comprehend that He would be rejected by His people or that He would willingly submit to suffering and death.

> *He is despised and rejected of men; a man of sorrows, and acquainted with grief: and we hid as it were our faces from him; he was despised, and we esteemed him not. Surely he hath borne our griefs, and carried our sorrows: yet we did esteem him stricken, smitten of God, and afflicted. But he was wounded for our transgressions, he was bruised for our iniquities: the chastisement of our peace*

*was upon him; and with his stripes we are healed. All we like sheep have gone astray; we have turned every one to his own way; and the LORD hath laid on him the iniquity of us all.* (Isaiah 53:3-6)

As the crowd passed by where Bartimaeus sat he heard someone say that Jesus of Nazareth was passing by. He had heard others talk about the miracles of Jesus, and it gave him hope that a miracle might be possible for him, so he began to shout, *". . . Jesus, thou Son of David, have mercy on me."* (Mark 10:47). Members of the crowd began to tell him to be quiet, for fear that those who were plotting against Jesus would hear. But he couldn't be quiet. He couldn't let this once in a lifetime opportunity pass by; it was now or never, so he shouted even louder, *". . . Thou Son of David, have mercy on me."* (v.48). When Jesus heard him, He stood still and commanded that Bartimaeus be brought to Him. Hearing this, the crowd told Bartimaeus, *". . . Be of good comfort, rise; he calleth thee"*. (v.49). This was music to his ears and he quickly cast his heavy cloak aside and began to grope his way to Jesus. The crowd was now parting to make the way clear. Someone took him by the arm and led him to Jesus, who said, *". . . What wilt thou that I should do unto thee?"* (v.51a). His answer was simple and direct, *". . . Lord, that I might receive my sight."* (v.51b).

The miracle came without any incantation being uttered. There was no stroke of lightning or peal of thunder, but it was instantaneous: *"And Jesus said unto him, Go thy way; thy faith hath made thee whole. And immediately he received his sight. . ."* (v.52a). As the darkness receded, tears came to his eyes and he blinked at the brightness. Light, beautiful, glorious, light flooded into his life bringing form and shape into the dark void of his existence. His universe was now illuminated with all the colors of the rainbow. Then, immediately in front of him, he could see the face that he had longed to see. It was the face of his Savior, the face of God in human flesh, Jesus! He could have stood there, just looking at that face for an eternity. But, wait a minute, what was it He had said? *"Go thy way; thy faith hath made thee whole. . ."*. But which way was he to go? He thought a moment, then he knew, there was only one way, so he *". . . followed Jesus in the way."* (v.52b).

All the way to Jerusalem Bartimaeus was constantly exclaiming to anyone who would listen, about what he saw. The sky, the palm trees, the rocks, the sand, even the footprints in the dust of the road were beautiful to him. The textures of people's robes, their appearance, they way they walked or gestured, all were new to him. And, most startling of all, were the colors. For the first time, he saw tan, gray, green, yellow, red, but the most wonderful of all was the blue that filled the canopy overhead. He had heard the word *sky* but he had never really known what it was. Now he saw it and it was glorious; clouds only served to make the blue more intense. When evening came and he saw his first sunset, he was enthralled with its beauty. When night came it made him a little nervous, until the stars began to twinkle overhead proving that it was not an absolute darkness, such as he had known for so long. Then, morning and sunrise, this would become his favorite sight. The gradual growing light of the new day that began with the graying of the sky, followed by a riot of color filled with the promise of a new beginning.

What else did Bartimaeus see? Surely he must have watched as Jesus rode a colt into Jerusalem, while the crowd spread their cloaks on the ground, waved palm branches, and shouted *"Hosanna"*. His eyes may have witnessed the horrors of the crucifixion as Jesus, nailed to the cross, gave His life so that we might be redeemed. Surely he was present in the crowd of believers, after the resurrection, watching as Jesus ascended up in the clouds. There he would have seen and heard the angels as they spoke to the crowd, *". . . Ye men of Galilee, why stand ye gazing up into heaven? this same Jesus, which is taken up from you into heaven, shall so come in like manner as ye have seen him go into heaven."* (Acts 1:11)

MILEPOSTS-

**Bartimaeus' Belief-** When he called out, *". . . Jesus, thou Son of David, have mercy on me."* (v.47b) He was demonstrating that though he was blind physically, he was not spiritually blind. He was acknowledging Jesus as the Messiah, the Savior. Bartimaeus also asked Jesus to have mercy on him. That is what we all need, the mercy of God which is granted to us through faith in Jesus as our Savior.

**Bartimaeus' Boldness-** He refused to be quiet because he was desperate and he knew that passing before him was the One, the only One who could help him. We have to recognize our desperation before we can really call on Jesus for help. *"Let us therefore come boldly unto the throne of grace, that we may obtain mercy, and find grace to help in time of need."* (Hebrews 4:16)

**Bartimaeus' Blessing**- *"And Jesus said unto him, Go thy way; thy faith hath made thee whole. And immediately he received his sight, and followed Jesus in the way"* (Mark 10:52). Bartimaeus focus was changed from darkness to light. His purpose was changed from begging to praise. And, he went from sitting and begging to following Jesus.

**The Worst Blindness-** We don't like even to think about being blind and living in darkness. But there is something worse, to live in spiritual blindness. Most people are living in a world of darkness without the light of God in their lives. The only cure is to believe in Jesus as your Savior and receive Him into your life. *"Then spake Jesus again unto them, saying, I am the light of the world: he that followeth me shall not walk in darkness, but shall have the light of life."* (John 8:12)

## 15

# The Road to Jericho

*"...A certain man went down from Jerusalem to Jericho..."* (Luke 10:30)

He had arisen early in the morning to prepare for this trip. Gathering everything he would need in a pack, he threw it on his back, said goodbye to his family and began walking on the road to the city of Jericho. As he left Jerusalem, he turned and looked back, marveling at the beauty of the city on the hill. The Temple glowed with a golden hue, awash with the rays of the rising sun. It was a magnificent sight. As he passed by the Mount of Olives, he saw the large grove of olive trees and the press which extracted oil from the olives. Later in the day, he would long for the shade of those trees. It was a good day for traveling, though, and he was enjoying the walk.

He was going to Jericho, the oldest and lowest city in the world. The seventeen mile trip would take most of the day, and was downhill all the way. The climb back up, however, would be much more difficult. At 853 feet below sea level, Jericho is 3,000 feet lower than Jerusalem. As he passed by Bethany the sun had risen higher in the sky and it began to grow

## The Road to Jericho

warm. It would grow even warmer before he reached his destination. Because of its low altitude, Jericho enjoyed near tropical temperatures the year around. Even when it snowed in the Judean highlands, it was still warm and pleasant in Jericho. For this reason, Herod had built his winter palace there, so he could spend his winters in comfort.

Located on the edge of a fertile plain, situated near the red rock cliffs of the Jordan River Valley and watered by springs that came down out of the mountains, including the Spring of Elisha, Jericho was an oasis. It was called *The City of Palms* for the numerous Palm trees that surrounded the city. Balsam trees grew there, as well. The resin of the Balsams was collected and sold for use as incense and in medicinal compounds. That was the reason Arah was making this trip. An apothecary, he needed balsam for making ointments and in order to purchase it he was carrying more money than he usually did.

Now, as the dusty road descended toward the Plains of Jordan which border the Judean Desert, it followed alongside the Wadi Qelt, a deep, dark canyon that many have identified with the *Valley of the Shadow of Death* mentioned by David in the 23rd Psalm. Traveling alone was risky, but Arah had been in too much of a hurry to wait for a group of travelers to accompany him. As he walked along beside the deep dark declivity, he wished there were other travelers to keep him company. He heard noises, was it his imagination? Perhaps he had been rash in deciding to come alone.

Soon, he would be down to the spot where he could see the plains and the city. From that point on, it would be much safer. Suddenly, as he rounded a turn in the road, a band of ruffians jumped out from behind a boulder. He reached for the sword that hung from his belt but they had spotted him first and rushed him, beating him with clubs and their fists before he could draw his sword. His head swimming, he stumbled and fell on the dusty trail. The thieves ripped the pack from his back, kicked him into the ditch beside the road, and fled.

> *. . . A certain man went down from Jerusalem to Jericho, and fell among thieves, which stripped him of his raiment, and wounded him, and departed, leaving him half dead.* (Luke 10:30)

For some time, how long he could not tell, he drifted into and out of consciousness. He had been severely injured and the hot sun was draining his body of moisture and strength. Without help he could not possibly survive. His family would be left in a desperate condition without him to provide for them.

A priest came by, going home to Jordan after finishing his service in the Temple at Jerusalem. He saw the man lying beside the road, but, thinking he was dead, did not trouble himself to check, but passed on by because he was anxious to get home and enjoy his time off from service.

> *And by chance there came down a certain priest that way: and when he saw him, he passed by on the other side.* (Luke 10:31)

Later, a Levite, on his way to serve in Jerusalem, stopped and looked at Arah. He seemed too far gone to be helped. If he was dead and the Levite touched him, he would not be eligible to do his work in the Temple for this round. So, he too, passed on by on the other side of the road, more concerned about serving in the Temple than in helping an injured fellow Jew.

*And likewise a Levite, when he was at the place, came and looked on him, and passed by on the other side.* (Luke 10:32)

As the sun soared overhead, the heat continued to drain Arah's body of moisture and he grew weaker as the hours passed. In a waking moment, he began to pray by reciting the words of David the Psalmist, *"Yea, though I walk through the valley of the shadow of death, I will fear no evil: for thou art with me..."* (Psalm 23:4a). Then he heard the braying of a donkey. Someone else was coming along the road. If only this person would be someone with enough compassion to help, then he still might survive, thought Arah as he lapsed again into unconsciousness.

A man's voice awakened him again and Arah found himself looking into the face of a stranger, who was telling him that he would apply medication and take him where he would be safe. He felt gentle hands touching him as bandages were wrapped around his wounds. Then his head was lifted up and a bottle placed to his parched lips. He drank of the sweetest wine he had ever tasted. There was something different about the stranger's appearance, he did not quite look like a Jew. Then it dawned upon Arah, the stranger was a Samaritan. The Jews and Samaritans had no dealing with each other and avoided contact as much as they could. But Arah was too weak and in need of help to object.

*But a certain Samaritan, as he journeyed, came where he was: and when he saw him, he had compassion on him, And went to him, and bound up his wounds, pouring in oil and wine, and set him on his own beast, and brought him to an inn, and took care of him.* (Luke 10:33-34)


MILEPOSTS-

**The Good Samaritan** - This parable was given in response to a question asked of Jesus by a lawyer i.e. one who knows and interprets the religious Law. He asked what he could do to inherit eternal life. Jesus told him the parable and then asked which character was a neighbor to the victim of the thieves. When the lawyer replied, *"He that showed mercy on him."* Jesus told him, *"Go, and do thou likewise"*. Life's problems present us with a choice. We can come along side others and help them, or we can just ignore the situation.

**Parables** - A *parable* is a story that *parallels* real life and is given to illustrate a particular point. The parable of the Good Samaritan was like a mirror, reflecting the attitudes and behavior of the religious leaders of the day. Is there any part of us reflected in this same mirror? Which character in the parable is a reflection of the way we live our lives?

**Abandoned on Life's Highway** - Satan robs and wounds people, leaving them in a drastic condition. Society, at large, ignores the victims of sin. Jesus, the Great Physician has compassion for them. He binds up their wounds and restores hope in their lives.

**Neighbor** - The word *neighbor* is derived from an old English word "neahgebur" meaning someone near your dwelling. We don't have to go a long way from home or search far to find someone who needs our help and our prayers.

**Israel's Neighbors** - Today, the nation of Israel resembles the man who was left alone on the highway. Israel is surrounded on all sides by its enemies. Who will be its helper and friend? Remember that God told Abraham: *"And I will bless them that bless thee, and curse him that curseth thee: and in thee shall all families of the earth be blessed."* (Genesis 12:3)

(Note: I used literary license in retelling the parable and I chose Arah for the main character's name because it means "Traveler" in Hebrew)

# 16

# Traveling the Same Road Twice

*". . . and took his journey into a far country"*
(Luke 15:13b)

It had seemed so easy the first time. Then it was all downhill. New sights to see; new things discovered around every bend in the road. A whole new world that had only existed in tales told back on the farm. Ahian's steps were light and he had not a care in the world. He was as free as the wind; all the burden of work and responsibility left behind. He went at his own pace, wherever his steps led. He walked when he felt like it and stopped wherever things attracted him. He didn't have to answer to anyone, least of all his conscience. His knapsack seemed light, though it was filled with all he possessed. Then, he was out to see the world. Now, he is retreating from it.

The road seems to be all uphill as he retraces familiar territory. His steps drag with the weight of regret. The pack on his back is empty, but it is heavy with remorse. The home that he had been so happy to leave, beckons him as his last hope in the world. What had seemed like a good idea at the time, now appears as the most foolish thing he has ever done. The road stretches endlessly before him and the miles, returning, seem twice as long as they were going. It is the same road, but he is traveling in the opposite direction.

It all began when some of his friends visited his father's farm. They were filled with excitement and were anxious tell about the sights they had seen and the adventures they had while traveling. Their stories awakened in him a desire to see the world and partake of its pleasures. Ahian had never been anywhere or seen anything except what existed on the farm. He yearned for travel and adventure. He wanted to experience life on a different level. This is natural, and to be expected in a young man, but his plan for accomplishing it was not the best idea he ever had.

As he thought about it, he realized that it would require money and he had none. He knew that, someday, he and his older brother would inherit their father's estate. He did not care to follow in his father's footsteps and become a farmer, so why not ask his father to give him his share now? With money, he could go to new places and learn new things. He could become more sophisticated and find a way of life that suited him. The more he turned it over in his mind, the more reasonable it seemed, at least to him.

Finally, Ahian went to his father and made the brash proposal that since he was dissatisfied with the way things were, why not let him have his share of the estate now? *"And the younger of them said to his father, Father, give me the portion of goods that falleth to me. . . "* (Luke 15:12a). Eventually, realizing his son's dissatisfaction and knowing he could not keep him at home forever, his father relented, *". . . And he divided unto them his living."* (Luke 15:12). Though the father's heart was heavy, he hoped that his son would learn the lessons that only experience and hardship teach.

It didn't take long for Ahian to put his plan into effect, *"And not many days after the younger son gathered all together, and took his journey into a far country, and there wasted his substance with riotous living."* (Luke 15:13) He met lots of new people and it was easy to make friends, since he was so generous with his wealth. Whatever amusement they suggested was fine with him and he paid the bill. People flocked to him like bees to honey. His popularity knew no bounds, and he was invited to every party. He scarcely noted his descent into coarser and coarser amusements. It was all new and adventurous to him. He reveled in it. He wallowed in it. What an improvement, he thought, over his former life. His family back home didn't know what they were missing, though he scarcely ever gave them a thought. Occasionally, he did seem to notice that his funds were diminishing, but then along came another friend with some new and exciting idea to try.

Then one day, as he awoke with a throbbing head, he glanced into his purse and was shocked to see that it was nearly empty. It had gone so fast. He searched around his room, thinking that perhaps some was left in reserve. But, no even what he had kept for a rainy day had been spent. With rising panic, he searched again, but turned up only a few coins that had been overlooked. Now, when friends came by he made excuses for not going with them. At first, they tried to persuade him, then their visits became less frequent, as they perceived that he no longer had money to throw away. He was no longer fun to be with. He grew sullen and introspective, avoiding all company, except when asking for a favor.

When Ahian could no longer pay his rent, he was ejected from his room and had to live with some of his few remaining friends until he wore out his welcome. His descent was gradual at first, but gained speed and his condition worsened. Now living on the street, he sought whatever work would pay for food to sustain him another day. Finally, at rock bottom, he agreed to tend a farmer's hogs. He knew this was a violation of his Jewish heritage, but he was desperate.

Feeling the pangs of an empty stomach, he began to look around and take in his surroundings. He was living in a pig sty without much hope of anything better. The hogs fared better than he did. Ahian went from being *sick of home* to being *homesick*. *"And when he came to himself, he said, How many hired servants of my father's have bread enough and to spare, and I perish with hunger! I will arise and go to my father, and will say unto him, Father, I have sinned against heaven, and before thee, And am no more worthy to be called thy son: make me as one of thy hired servants."* (Luke 15:17-19)

As he traveled the same road back home, his heart was heavy with remorse, and a tear flowed for each wrong he had done. He had cared nothing for his family, and disrespected his father. He repented of all the sins he so freely committed in leaving home and living a prodigal life. There were no delusions about what sort of reception he might receive. It would be enough if he would be permitted to become a servant in his father's house. As he turns into the lane that leads home, he marvels at how beautiful the countryside now appears. Sights that once seemed distasteful in their familiarity now beckon him homeward. Memories that once seemed dull now are precious. Each rock, fencepost and each stream are old familiar friends. Just a little farther and he will be there. Home will no longer be a prison but a refuge.

Rounding the last bend in the road, he sees a figure in the distance. He had hoped to just sort of sneak in among the servants and gradually make his presence known, but he has been spotted. His steps falter when he realizes it is his father. He tries to shrink into himself, dreading the confrontation he is sure awaits, but willing to humble himself and grovel if necessary. His only hope is to ask for mercy. What's this? His father is running toward him with a smile on his face. Throwing his arms around his wayward son, he weeps for joy. Instead of a lecture, he welcomes him with the joy only a father can know, when his lost child is restored to him.

> *And he arose, and came to his father. But when he was yet a great way off, his father saw him, and had compassion, and ran, and fell on his neck, and kissed him. And the son said unto him, Father, I have sinned against heaven, and in thy sight, and am no more worthy to be called thy son. But the father said to his servants, Bring forth the best robe, and put it on him; and put a ring on his hand, and shoes on his feet: And bring hither the*

*fatted calf, and kill it; and let us eat, and be merry: For this my son was dead, and is alive again; he was lost, and is found. And they began to be merry.* (Luke 15:20-24)

As the celebration proceeds, the sounds of merrymaking carry into the field where his older brother, Ahikam, is working. This is unusual and seems out of place. He returns to the house, and calls one of the servants to inquire. The servant informs him that his younger brother has returned and his father is welcoming him home with a celebration. Far from being pleased at his brother's return, Ahikam is resentful and when approached by his father, his anger spills over. He tells his father that he has been the faithful son and has worked for him many years. The father's reply puts things in their proper perspective:

*And he said unto him, Son, thou art ever with me, and all that I have is thine. It was meet that we should make merry, and be glad: for this thy brother was dead, and is alive again; and was lost, and is found.* (Luke 15:31-32)

MILEPOSTS-

**Separation-** Separation from God brings sorrow and suffering. He created us for fellowship with Him and there is no contentment apart from Him. *"For a day in thy courts is better than a thousand. I had rather be a doorkeeper in the house of my God, than to dwell in the tents of wickedness."* (Psalm 84:10)

**The Heart of a Father-** It is wonderful to know that God has love and compassion for His created beings. *"Like as a father pitieth his children, so the LORD pitieth them that fear him."* (Psalm 103:13)

**The Welcome-** Just as the father received his wayward son with joy, so God the Father delights in the return of His children; *I say unto you, that likewise joy shall be in heaven over one sinner that repenteth, more than over ninety and nine just persons, which need no repentance.* (Luke 15:7)

**The Point of the Parable-** The Parable of the Prodigal Son is a beautiful story of redemption, but it has a point that is often overlooked. The Pharisees felt they were entitled to Heaven simply because they were descendants of Abraham and had criticized Jesus for receiving sinners. Jesus told this story to make it clear that those who come, humbly, repenting of their sins, are the true heirs of the Kingdom. Entrance to Heaven isn't gained as a result of our ancestry or by *being good* but through the free gift of God's grace, given to those who accept Jesus as their Savior. Those who rejected Jesus were rejecting the God the Father. Those who accept Him are the true *children of Abraham* and the heirs of the Promise.

> **Note:** Since this is a Parable, which is a story told to illustrate a point, and not a historical incident, I felt free to be more imaginative in telling the story. The two sons were given names based upon the way they conducted themselves. The name of the prodigal, Ahian

means, in Hebrew, *brother of wine*. The older son's name, Ahikam means *a brother who raises up, or avenges*.

# 17

# The Road Less Traveled

*And he was sad at that saying, and went away grieved: for he had great possessions.* (Mark 10:22)

The clinking of gold coins was the only sound in the counting house as the old man counted his wealth and carefully marked it down in his account book. The gold had lost none of its luster since he had inherited it from his father, a wealthy merchant, many years ago. As a young man he had loved the feel of it, its bright gleam in the lamplight, and had reveled in the stacks of it piled up high. He had received a fortune from his father's estate, but had also worked hard and saved diligently to add to it over the years. Loving money more than anything else in the world, he had sacrificed family and friendship to accumulate more. The challenge of getting it was his chief delight. His pursuit of gold had been ruthless, and it grieved him to part with even the least of it.

With the coming of old age, though, something had changed. Gold never loses its shine, since it doesn't rust or corrode, yet it didn't seem as bright as it once had. Was it his eyes, dimmed by age that made the difference? Or was it because he was beginning to understand that he had missed out on something else that was very important. Sitting among his treasure, his thoughts began to wander back to the time of his youth, when anything seemed possible. The world held great promise and he had every advantage to attain it. However, he wondered if there was something beyond all that the world had to offer.

When he was young, someone told him of a man who taught as no one else had ever taught. Others taught that it was necessary to keep every letter of the law, and observe every ritual. There were so many regulations that it would occupy most of one's time in trying to be good enough to merit Heaven, and the least fault would keep one out of Heaven. This teacher, whose name was Jesus, spoke of God as His Father, and taught that going to Heaven depended on having a personal relationship with God. It was reported that He had healed the sick, restored sight to the blind and brought the dead back to life. The rich young man decided that he must meet that teacher. He had a question to ask Him.

One day, hearing that Jesus was in the area, the rich young ruler wasted no time in going to meet Him and asking his question:

*And when he was gone forth into the way, there came one running, and kneeled to him, and asked him, Good Master, what shall I do that I may inherit eternal life?* (Mark 10:17)

The answer he received startled him. It sounded like what he was already trying to do, not something out of the ordinary:

*And Jesus said unto him, Why callest thou me good? there is none good but one, that is, God. Thou knowest the commandments, Do not commit adultery, Do not kill, Do not steal, Do not bear false witness, Defraud not, Honour thy father and mother.* (Mark 10:18-19)

He was proud of his efforts at keeping the law and commandments. He truly thought that he was a righteous person:

*And he answered and said unto him, Master, all these have I observed from my youth.* (Mark 10:20)

Maybe this wasn't so difficult after all. This was basically what the Jewish leaders taught. "Maybe, if I kept the law and commandments then I would be qualified for Heaven by my works." He felt pleased with himself, until Jesus said something else:

*Then Jesus beholding him loved him, and said unto him, One thing thou lackest: go thy way, sell whatsoever thou hast, and give to the poor, and thou shalt have treasure in heaven: and come, take up the cross, and follow me.* (Mark 10:21)

Nothing could have surprised the rich young ruler more than that. He, like many others believed that having wealth was an indication of God's favor. He thought that if you were good, then God blessed you with much and if you weren't good, then you didn't receive as much. To be told to sell all he had and give to the poor went against everything he believed. He loved his money and possessions. It would break his heart to give them up. And what was that business about taking up a cross? The cross was shameful to any Roman or Jewish citizen. He decided right then and there that the price was too high:

*And he was sad at that saying, and went away grieved: for he had great possessions.* (Mark 10:22)

The years had passed by and the Rich Young Ruler was now the Rich Old Ruler. He had discovered that his wealth had not brought him happiness. There was still an empty spot in his heart. He still longed for something he did not have. As he reflected on his youth and the words Jesus had spoken to him, he wondered if the offer was still open. Could he at this late date still choose to follow Jesus? Or was it too late?

MILEPOSTS-

**The Burden of Wealth -** The more you possess, the more time and effort you have to put into maintaining those things. Even money has to be looked after, or you will lose it. *"A good name is rather to* *be chosen than great riches, and loving favour rather than silver and gold."* (Proverbs 22:1)

**The Purpose of Life -** Life's purpose is not to accumulate things, but to live out God's will for your life. *"Lay not up for yourselves treasures upon earth, where moth and rust doth corrupt, and where thieves break through and steal: But lay up for yourselves treasures in heaven, where neither moth nor rust doth corrupt, and where thieves do not break through nor steal: For where your treasure is, there will your heart be also."* (Matthew 6:19-21)

**The Road Less Traveled -** To follow Jesus is to be in the minority. *"Because strait is the gate, and narrow is the way, which leadeth unto life, and few there be that find it."* (Matthew 7:14). The majority of people are not willing to give up that which they cannot keep (wealth or power) to gain that which you cannot lose (eternal life). Not many people are willing to take the Cross road.

**The Cross -** Salvation is free, but it cost Jesus His death on the cross. The cross means sacrifice. If we desire to follow Him then we must be willing to sacrifice everything for His sake. Jesus told the Rich Young Ruler to sell everything and give it away because his money had become his idol. Anything that takes precedence over God in your life is an idol. *"Then said Jesus unto his disciples, If any man will come after me, let him deny himself, and take up his cross, and follow me."* (Matthew 16:24)

**Don't Wait Until It Is Too Late** - Many have put off giving their heart and lives to Jesus until it was too late. We have no promise of tomorrow. We have only today in which to make our decision. *"Seek ye the LORD while he may be found, call ye upon him while he is near:"* (Isaiah 55:6)

# 18

# The Cross Road

*"And as they came out, they found a man of Cyrene, Simon by name: him they compelled to bear his cross."* (Matthew 27:32)

As he walked the streets of Jerusalem, Simon was elated and thankful that he had finally been able to make the trip to the Holy City. He was among the many Jews who had made the pilgrimage to be present during Passover week. One of ten thousand Jews who had settled in the city of Cyrene, on the coast of North Africa, he had long desired to see the city and celebrate the Passover here. He toured the city, enjoying the sights which held historical as well as religious significance for every descendant of Abraham, including, of course, the temple which was the center of Jewish worship.

The temple that Simon saw was not the original temple, however. The first one, built by Solomon, had been destroyed by Nebuchadnezzar. Rebuilt by Zerubbabel, after the Babylonian Captivity, the second one had fallen into disrepair until it was restored and enlarged by Herod the Great. The temple Herod built was a magnificent, eye dazzling, structure of white marble, its front adorned with gold; its grounds, including several courtyards covered an area of 35 acres. This was a sight every Jew longed to see. Simon stood for a long time looking at it in wonder and awe. Whenever he came into the city during the next few days, his gaze would return to the temple mount.

The Jews were proud of their temple, even the Disciples were willing to boast about it. But Jesus prophesied that it would one day be destroyed: *"And as some spake of the temple, how it was adorned with goodly stones and gifts, he said, As for these things which ye behold, the days will come, in the which there shall not be left one stone upon another, that shall not be thrown down."* (Luke 21:5-6). His prophecy was fulfilled, when in 70 AD the Jews revolted against the Romans. They responded by crushing the revolt and destroying the Temple. More than a million Jews perished. Those who managed to escape scattered across the earth, but they have never lost hope that, one day, the temple will be rebuilt, once again. The only part left standing today is the western, or *Wailing* wall.

Simon had arrived in Jerusalem just the previous week. For many years he had dreamed about making this pilgrimage. When the time was right everything fell into place. Once his plans were made and provisions gathered, Simon had gone to the seaport of Apollonia and booked passage on a Roman ship. He had to carry his own food with him since none was provided. At night he rolled out his blankets on deck, regardless of whether the stars were shining or a storm was threatening; this was no luxury cruise. The ship sailed over 700 miles to Caesarea Maritima, which had the largest harbor on the Mediterranean, another of Herod's building projects. When he landed from the ship, Simon still faced a walk of 70 miles to reach his destination. The road was dangerous, infested with hijackers and thieves. Since it was the Passover season, there were many others making the same pilgrimage, so he was able to join one of their caravans for the trek south. A large number of Cyrenians lived near Jerusalem and they had even built a synagogue there. When Simon arrived, he was able to stay with some of them in the country just outside the city.

Early Friday morning he went into Jerusalem. Always crowded during Passover and the feast of Unleavened Bread, which lasted for seven days, the city was filled with people. On this day they seemed to be agitated. Some were angry and shouting, others were weeping. Simon was puzzled. The mood of the crowd was not one of celebration as it should be during the feast. He found himself standing on the street in front of the Fortress Antonia, on the northwest side of the temple mount. This is where the Roman governors stayed when they came down from their official residence in Caesarea. Pilate was here during the Passover to maintain order among the Jews.

Simon watched, wondering what was going on. Soldiers were stationed at intervals along the sides of the street. Presently, a procession appeared, coming out from the Praetorium, or courtyard of the fortress. Three men were stumbling along the pavement, each one surrounded by four soldiers. Each man carrying a cross. Simon realized, to his horror, that this was an execution procession. The third man had obviously

## The Cross Road

been beaten horribly. He wore a crown made of thorns on his head. As he drew alongside where Simon was standing, he stumbled and fell under the weight of his cross, too weak to carry it any farther. Suddenly, Simon felt a touch on his shoulder. A Roman soldier had tapped him with his spear, ordering him to pick up the cross of the fallen man. In a daze, he did as he was commanded. He was forced to march along with the condemned men. Passing through a gate in the city wall, they marched toward the place of execution, which was on a nearby hill. As they approached it, Simon could see that a rock formation in the side of the hill resembled a human skull. Then he heard someone call it Golgotha, which means *skull* in Hebrew (in Latin, it is Calvary).

When they came to the top of the hill, Simon was forced to drop the cross on the ground. Then he was shoved back into the crowd of spectators. He was relieved to be rid of his burden. Not wanting to witness an execution, he moved to the back of the crowd where he wouldn't have to see what was happening. Still, he could hear the anguished cries of the men as they were thrown down on their crosses. Then he heard the sound of hammers as the soldiers drove long spikes through the men's hands and feet, fastening them to their crosses. Two of the men were cursing the soldiers, but the third one said,

> "... *Father, forgive them; for they know not what they do...*" (Luke 23:34).

As the crosses were lifted and dropped into holes in the ground, Simon could see the men. Over the head of the one in the middle, the soldiers nailed a sign, *"And a superscription also was written over him in letters of Greek, and Latin, and Hebrew, THIS IS THE KING OF THE JEWS."* (Luke 23:38) The sign had been ordered by Pilate. It was written in three languages so everyone could read it. Hebrew was the language of the Jews. Greek was the universal language spoken by much of the world, as English is in our time. Latin was the official language of the Roman Empire. The inscription is often seen on crosses and crucifixes today, abbreviated as INRI for the Latin words, "Iesus Nazarenus, Rex Iudaeorum" which, in English is, "Jesus the Nazarene King of the Jews".

As he looked into the eyes of that man, Simon realized that these were not the eyes of a criminal. His heart was moved with compassion as he wondered why this man was being crucified. Curious to find out, he felt compelled to stay and see what else might happen. The soldiers sat down to wait for the men to die, and passed the time gambling for the clothes of the man on the middle cross. People were passing by on the road, which was a busy thoroughfare. When they saw what was happening on the hill, they shouted in derision, *". . . Ah, thou that destroyest the temple, and buildest it in three days, Save thyself, and come down from the cross."* (Mark 15:29-30).

Why, Simon wondered, was all this ridicule aimed at the man on the central cross? What had he done to incur such extreme wrath? The other two were criminals, condemned for their deeds, but the one in the middle did not appear to be like them at all. Then, they all began to speak:

*The Cross Road*

*And one of the malefactors which were hanged railed on him, saying, If thou be Christ, save thyself and us. But the other answering rebuked him, saying, Dost not thou fear God, seeing thou art in the same condemnation? And we indeed justly; for we receive the due reward of our deeds: but this man hath done nothing amiss. And he said unto Jesus, Lord, remember me when thou comest into thy kingdom. And Jesus said unto him, Verily I say unto thee, To day shalt thou be with me in paradise.* (Luke 23:39-43)

So, one of the criminals seemed to think this man was innocent. This was becoming more intriguing every minute. There were some women standing nearby and the man in the middle spoke again:

*Now there stood by the cross of Jesus his mother, and his mother's sister, Mary the wife of Cleophas, and Mary Magdalene. When Jesus therefore saw his mother, and the disciple standing by, whom he loved, he saith unto his mother, Woman, behold thy son! Then saith he to the disciple, Behold thy mother! And from that hour that disciple took her unto his own home.* (John 19:25-27)

It was now midday, but the sun suddenly dimmed, and a chilling darkness fell over the land. What was this all about? Why were all these strange things happening? Simon was tired and his emotions were stretched to the breaking point, but he couldn't bring himself to leave. He sat down, determined to watch and listen until it was all over. Three more hours passed, then the man on the central cross was speaking again,

> *And about the ninth hour Jesus cried with a loud voice, saying, Eli, Eli, lama sabachthani? that is to say, My God, my God, why hast thou forsaken me?* (Matthew 27:46)

For six hours, Simon had remained at the site of the crucifixion. Sweltering in the hot sun and faint from thirst, he knew that it had to be much worse for the three men on the crosses, as the heat drew moisture from their tortured bodies. The man who had captured his attention seemed to be near the end of his ordeal. His voice barely audible, through parched lips, he said,

> *. . . I thirst. Now there was set a vessel full of vinegar: and they filled a spunge with vinegar, and put it upon hyssop, and put it to his mouth.* (John 19 28-29)

His strength was rapidly waning, but after he had received the vinegar, which was mingled with spice, he exclaimed quite clearly,

> *When Jesus therefore had received the vinegar, he said, It is finished. . .* (John 19:30)

The long hours of suffering were now drawing to a close, and he uttered his final words in a loud voice,

*". . . he said, Father, into thy hands I commend my spirit: and having said thus, he gave up the ghost."* (Luke 23:46)

The Roman soldiers in charge of the crucifixion were under the command of a Centurion, *"And when the centurion, which stood over against him, saw that he so cried out, and gave up the ghost, he said, Truly this man was the Son of God."* (Mark 15:39)

It was growing late in the day and sundown would be the beginning of the Jewish Sabbath. The bodies could not be allowed to remain on the crosses. The soldiers, therefore began to break the legs of the men. This would ensure that they died, by suffocation, since they would no longer be able to lift themselves up to breathe. When they came to the one Simon was so intrigued by, they found he was already dead and did not break his legs. As a final act to the gory day, a soldier pierced his side with a spear. Blood and water flowed out. Then the bodies of the three men were taken down off the crosses and prepared for burial.

It was over, and time for Simon to leave this wretched site. As he started down the hill, the ground began to shake. It trembled so hard that he nearly lost his footing. Grabbing hold of a bush that grew nearby, he held on for dear life. Rocks were crashing down the hill and the air was filled with dust. It was only for only a few moments, but it seemed like forever. Finally, as suddenly as the quake began, the earth heaved one last time, and the tumult ceased. All was quiet once again. Making his way carefully to the bottom of the hill he discovered that the ground had opened up like a furrow made by a plow. The rock underneath was now exposed and he could see that it had been split apart, *". . . and the earth did quake, and the rocks rent"* (Matthew 27:51b).

Simon walked away with a heavy heart. This was not what he had come to Jerusalem to see. He had come for a joyous celebration, but had been forced to be present at a horrible execution. It was impossible to forget what he had seen, and the words he had heard kept echoing in his ears. There had to be more to the story of the man on the middle cross and he was determined to learn more about Him.

**The Rest of the Story -**

In writing the story above, I have tried to imagine how Simon of Cyrene came to be in Jerusalem, how he got involved in carrying the cross of Jesus, and how he may have felt while observing the crucifixion. The facts of the crucifixion were taken directly from the Bible, and the "Seven Last Sayings from the Cross" are included in approximately the order in which they were spoken.

Little is known about Simon, but it seems that he did become a Christian because Mark mentions him in a way that would imply that he was well known among believers, *"And they compel one Simon a Cyrenian, who passed by, coming out of the country, the father of Alexander and Rufus, to bear his cross."* (Mark 15:21).

In the book of Acts, Luke mentions a teacher named Simeon, *"Now there were in the church that was at Antioch certain prophets and teachers; as Barnabas, and Simeon that was called Niger, and Lucius of Cyrene, and Manaen, which had been brought up with Herod the tetrarch, and Saul." (Acts 13:1)* The name Simeon is the same as Simon and the word Niger means black and could refer to the color of his hair (not his skin, as he was an expatriate Jew). Some scholars think the Lucius mentioned in this verse is actually the Luke, who wrote the Gospel. So, if that is the case, Luke and Simon would have known each other.

How about Simon's family? In the book of Romans, Paul mentions Rufus and his mother, *"Salute Rufus chosen in the Lord, and his mother and mine."* (Romans 16:13). This was very likely Simon's son mentioned in Mark 15:21. and his mother had been very kind and helpful to Paul, so that Paul mentions her as being as close to him as his own mother.

In 1941, during an excavation in the Kidron Valley, near Jerusalem, a number of ossuaries (stone boxes used to hold bones) were found in a tomb dating back to the first century A.D. On the side of one of the boxes was the inscription "Alexandros Simenos" which means "Alexander, son of Simon". Inscribed on the lid of the box were these words, "Alexandros Querinay" which means "Alexander of Cyernica".

MILEPOSTS-

**Why Did Jesus Have to Die?** - He was totally innocent. He had never committed a single sin, yet He died on the cross, as the perfect sacrifice, to pay the price for our sins. *"Much more then, being now justified by his blood, we shall be saved from wrath through him."* (Romans 5:9)

**God's Love for Us** - God loved us enough to give us the gift of His Son. *"For God so loved the world, that he gave his only begotten Son, that whosoever believeth in him should not perish, but have everlasting life. For God sent not his Son into the world to condemn the world; but that the world through him might be saved."* (John 3:16-17)

**Our Response to the Cross** - should be to receive Jesus into our hearts and lives and then to follow him by taking up our cross. *"Then said Jesus unto his disciples, If any man will come after me, let him deny himself, and take up his cross, and follow me."* (Matthew 16:24)

**Our Cross** - doesn't consist of the troubles we face in life. Our cross is to deny ourselves, which means to put Jesus first in all things. When we invite Him into our lives as Savior, we must allow Him to be the Lord of our daily living. When He is in control, He will work out the plan and purpose He has for our lives. Those who bear His cross on earth will receive a crown in Heaven.

## 19

# On the Road Again

*"And he said unto them, What manner of communications are these that ye have one to another, as ye walk, and are sad?"* (Luke 24:17)

It is a glorious Sunday afternoon, as two men walk slowly along the road leading northwest from the city. The sun is shining, birds are singing and flowers bloom in the fields alongside the road, but all that means nothing to the two companions. They are earnestly talking and disputing with one another regarding the events of the past week. They had gone up to Jerusalem for the celebration of the Passover and the Feast of Unleavened Bread, which should have been a joyous occasion but, instead, became the worst week of their lives.

It had all begun well, as they watched Jesus ride into Jerusalem on a donkey, the previous Sunday. They had been among those who waved palm branches and shouted *"Hosanna,"* anticipating that the time had come when He would lead them to cast off the cruel yoke of the Roman occupation. They were convinced that He was the long awaited Messiah. They had seen Him heal the sick, cause the lame to walk, and restore sight to the blind. They had heard Him speak of God as His Father, and say many things that were not like the sermons of the other rabbis, who always quoted someone else. When He spoke, it was as if God Himself was talking to them. Huge crowds followed Him everywhere He went, eager to listen to His words, *"For he taught them as one having authority, and not as the scribes."* (Matthew 7:29).

But then, their world began to fall apart. The religious rulers, jealous of Jesus' popularity, and fearful of losing their power, had Him arrested. He was subjected to trials by the Jewish authorities, by Herod, and finally by Pilate, the Roman governor. Pilate was not convinced that He was guilty of anything, *"Pilate therefore, willing to release Jesus, spake again to them. But they cried, saying, Crucify him, crucify him."* (Luke 23:20-21). Then they took Jesus, along with two criminals, to the hill of Golgotha and crucified them.

Jesus was dead. Joseph of Arimathaea had taken His body and buried it in his own tomb. Their hopes were buried that Friday, in a tomb sealed with a stone rolled over the door. The Feast of Unleavened Bread was over. So, with no reason to stay in Jerusalem, the two men were walking the seven miles to their home in the village of Emmaus. They had gone up with joy, but were returning in sorrow.

While they walked along the lonely road, deep in disappointment and lost hope, another traveler drew near and began to walk along with them. Then He spoke and said, *". . . What manner of communications are these that ye have one to another, as ye walk, and are sad?"* (Luke 24:17). They were amazed that anyone would not know about what had transpired so recently in Jerusalem, so the one whose name was Cleopas, answered, *". . . Art thou only a stranger in Jerusalem, and hast not known the things which are come to pass there in these days?"* (Luke 24:18). Then they proceeded to fill Him in on the events of Jesus' crucifixion three days ago. Some women among the believers had told them that they had found His tomb empty, and had seen angels who said that He was alive. His disciples had not seen Him, however, and could not believe that it was so.

To their surprise, the stranger said, *". . . O fools, and slow of heart to believe all that the prophets have spoken: Ought not Christ to have suffered these things, and to enter into his glory?"* (Luke 24:25-26). Then He began to remind them of the scriptures which had prophesied the sufferings of the Messiah. Luke does not record the specific scriptures He quoted, but, very likely, some of them were these:

*"And I will put enmity between thee and the woman, and between thy seed and her seed; it shall bruise thy head, and thou shalt bruise his heel."* (Genesis 3:15)

*". . . they pierced my hands and my feet."* (Psalm 22:16)

*"They part my garments among them, and cast lots upon my vesture."* (Psalm 22:18)

*". . . My God, my God, why hast thou forsaken me? . . . "* (Psalm 22:1)

*". . . in my thirst they gave me vinegar to drink."* (Psalm 69:21)

*"He is despised and rejected of men; a man of sorrows, and acquainted with grief: and we hid as it were our faces from him; he was despised, and we esteemed him not. Surely he hath borne our griefs, and carried our sorrows: yet we did esteem him stricken, smitten of God, and afflicted. But he was wounded for our transgressions, he was bruised for our iniquities: the chastisement of our peace was upon him; and with his stripes we are healed."* (Isaiah 53:3-5)

There are many more prophecies in the Old Testament regarding our Savior. These are just a few that He may have used to remind the two men of how the Messiah would come as a Suffering Servant to purchase our redemption on the cross of Calvary. Now, they were drawing near to Emmaus, and it was growing late in the day, so they prevailed upon the stranger (they still did not recognize Him) to stay with them. Then, as they sat down to dinner, He took bread, blessed it, broke it and gave to them. Suddenly, their eyes were opened and they recognized that the stranger was Jesus. In that instant, He vanished from their sight. He was alive and had been walking and talking with them all afternoon, but they had been so focused on their sorrow that they had failed to really see Him.

*And their eyes were opened, and they knew him; and he vanished out of their sight. And they said one to another, Did not our heart burn within us, while he talked with us by the way, and while he opened to us the scriptures? And they rose up the same hour, and returned to Jerusalem...* (Luke 24:31-33a)

Though it is late in the day, they cannot keep the news to themselves, so they rush the seven miles back the way they came. By the time they reach Jerusalem, it is after dark. They find the other Disciples hiding in an upper room. The doors are barred. They are in fear for their lives, knowing that the enemies of Jesus may hunt them down and imprison or kill them. Then, as they listen to this, another strange story from some who claim to have seen Him, He appears suddenly before their very eyes,

*And they told what things were done in the way, and how he was known of them in breaking of bread. And as they thus spake, Jesus himself stood in the midst of them, and saith unto them, Peace be unto you. But they were terrified and affrighted, and supposed that they had seen a spirit.* (Luke 24:35-37)

At first, they are terrified, but then they become convinced that He is alive, as He shows them the nail prints in His hands and feet. He asks for food and eats it in their presence, proving that He is not just a vision or a ghost, but a real live person, returned from the grave.

*And he said unto them, Why are ye troubled? and why do thoughts arise in your hearts? Behold my hands and my feet, that it is I myself: handle me, and see; for a spirit hath not flesh and bones, as ye see me have. And when he had thus spoken, he shewed them his hands and his feet. And while they yet believed not for joy, and wondered, he said unto them, Have ye here any meat? And they gave him a piece of a broiled fish, and of an honeycomb. And he took it, and did eat before them.* (Luke 24:38-43)

Jesus then reminds them that He had told them, before it all happened, that He would die and rise again on the third day. Always slow to comprehend, the Disciples begin to understand how all the pieces fit together in the redemption story. Now that He has risen, and will be soon returning to the Father, it will be up to them to spread the Word. Jesus commissions them to begin where they are and preach the Gospel to all the world.

*And he said unto them, These are the words which I spake unto you, while I was yet with you, that all things must be fulfilled, which were written in the law of Moses, and in the prophets, and in the psalms, concerning me. Then opened he their understanding, that they might understand the scriptures, And said unto them, Thus it is written, and thus it behoved Christ to suffer, and to rise from the dead the third day: And that repentance and remission of sins should be preached in his name among all nations, beginning at Jerusalem. And ye are witnesses of these things.* (Luke 24:44-48)

The process of telling the world is still going on today as preachers proclaim the Good News to our country and missionaries preach it to all the world. The disciples on the Emmaus road said their hearts burned within them. God's servants today, with a flame in their hearts proclaim to the world that forgiveness of sin, and eternal life await all who will receive the living Lord Jesus into their hearts and lives.

MILEPOSTS-

**You can Participate in Christ's Resurrection** - The one thing most people fear is death. Down through the ages, the question has been asked, *"If a man die, shall he live again?..."* (Job 14:14a). Jesus answered that question when He arose from the grave, and made eternal life possible for anyone who will trust Him by faith, *"But now is Christ risen from the dead, and become the firstfruits of them that slept. For since by man came death, by man came also the resurrection of the dead. For as in Adam all die, even so in Christ shall all be made alive. But every man in his own order: Christ the firstfruits; afterward they that are Christ's at his coming."* (1 Corinthians 15:20-23)

**The Unseen Stranger -** Jesus is alive and still walks among us today, though many still do not recognize Him or receive Him into their hearts and lives. He forgives sin and gives eternal life to those who believe. He told the sister of Lazarus, *". . . I am the resurrection, and the life: he that believeth in me, though he were dead, yet shall he live: And whosoever liveth and believeth in me shall never die. Believest thou this?* (John 11:25-26)

**Past, Present, and Future -** The two on the road to Emmaus were dwelling on Jesus in the past. Don't leave Him in your past. Don't leave Him back there 2,000 years ago. He is alive today and He will walk with you today, tomorrow, and forever. We have His promise, *"Let your conversation be without covetousness; and be content with such things as ye have: for he hath said, I will never leave thee, nor forsake thee."* (Hebrews 13:5)

**How You Can Have a Home in Heaven-** Not only does He desire to walk with us in this world, but He wants us to be with Him forever, *"And if I go and prepare a place for you, I will come again, and receive you unto myself; that where I am, there ye may be also. And whither I go ye know, and the way ye know. Thomas saith unto him, Lord, we know not whither thou goest; and how can we know the way? Jesus saith unto him, I am the way, the truth, and the life: no man cometh unto the Father, but by me."* (John 14:3-6)

## 20

# Road to the Light

*"...but they led him by the hand, and brought him into Damascus."* (Acts 9:8b)

As the band of men walked along the hot, dusty road, rivulets of sweat running down their faces and muscles aching from their long journey, they were relieved to see that they were near Damascus. It had taken them 7 days to travel the 150 miles from Jerusalem. They had followed the Rift Valley, alongside the Jordan River, up past the Sea of Galilee to the region of Syria. Saul was carrying letters from the High Priest, authorizing him to arrest and bring to trial any followers of "The Way" that he found. The band consisted of Saul, and a contingent of soldiers who accompanied him to guard the prisoners he hoped to capture.

Saul had been born in Tarsus, a prominent city in Asia Minor. His father was a Jew who belonged to the strictest sect of the Pharisees, and had, somehow, obtained the position of citizenship in the Roman Empire. Saul had a sister and a nephew, who are mentioned in the book of Acts 23:16. As a young boy, Saul was given a good education and, according to Jewish custom, he was trained in a trade. His trade was that of tent making from goat's hair cloth, a common trade in Tarsus. When he came of age he was sent to Jerusalem to be educated in the school of Gamaliel, a renowned teacher of the Jewish law.

Later, he became aware of a Teacher who had become very popular with the people because He emphasized the love of God, rather than the traditions of the established Jewish leaders. This man had been crucified at the urging of the establishment, who feared an uprising of the common folks. His crucifixion, however, did not put an end to His influence. There had arisen a movement, the sect of the "Nazarenes", which later became known as "The Way". Their numbers were growing as their faith spread all over Jerusalem. Then, a man named Stephen began to preach that the Teacher, Jesus, was the Messiah. When he preached an especially powerful sermon, some of the crowd were incensed:

> *Then they cried out with a loud voice, and stopped their ears, and ran upon him with one accord, And cast him out of the city, and stoned him: and the witnesses laid down their clothes at a young man's feet, whose name was Saul. And they stoned Stephen, calling upon God, and saying, Lord Jesus, receive my spirit. And he kneeled down, and cried with a loud voice, Lord, lay not this sin to their charge. And when he had said this, he fell asleep. And Saul was consenting unto his death. And at that time there was a great persecution against the church which was*

*at Jerusalem; and they were all scattered abroad throughout the regions of Judaea and Samaria, except the apostles.* (Acts 7:58-8:1)

Saul continued to lead the persecution:. ". . . *he made havock of the church, entering into every house, and haling men and women committed them to prison. Therefore they that were scattered abroad went every where preaching the word.*" (Acts 8:3-4) Then, when he heard that some of the followers of "The Way" had fled to Damascus, in Syria, he set out to pursue them: *"And Saul, yet breathing out threatenings and slaughter against the disciples of the Lord, went unto the high priest, And desired of him letters to Damascus to the synagogues, that if he found any of this way, whether they were men or women, he might bring them bound unto Jerusalem."* (Acts 9:1-2)

The last leg of the journey was all uphill. When they reached the crest of a ridge, they paused to catch their breath and view Damascus, shimmering in the heat of the afternoon sun. There below them, on a plateau 2,230 feet above sea-level, lay one of the oldest cities in the world. With the Kassioun Mountain on the left and the Barada river flowing through the middle, it was an awesome sight. Two international highways, the Via Maris (Way of the Sea) and the Kings Highway ran through the city, a busy trading center filled with caravans from Egypt, to the south, and Mesopotamia, in the north.

Resuming their march, they were almost to their destination when it happened. A flash of light, brighter than the sun, hit them like a lightning bolt.

Saul and the men with him all fell to the ground. Saul would later tell the story of that day in his testimony to King Agrippa:

> *At midday, O king, I saw in the way a light from heaven, above the brightness of the sun, shining round about me and them which journeyed with me. And when we were all fallen to the earth, I heard a voice speaking unto me, and saying in the Hebrew tongue, Saul, Saul, why persecutest thou me? it is hard for thee to kick against the pricks. And I said, Who art thou, Lord? And he said, I am Jesus whom thou persecutest. But rise, and stand upon thy feet: for I have appeared unto thee for this purpose, to make thee a minister and a witness both of these things which thou hast seen, and of those things in the which I will appear unto thee; Delivering thee from the people, and from the Gentiles, unto whom now I send thee...* (Acts 26:13-17)

To his credit, Saul neither argued with nor questioned the Lord's command to him. In that flash of light, he had seen the truth. Jesus had indeed risen from the dead and had now chosen Saul, the chief persecutor of Christians, to become His ambassador to the world. Weakly he arose to his feet and opened his eyes but he saw nothing except darkness; he was blind. The men with him took him by the hand and led him, like a little child, into the city of Damascus, where he stayed in the house of a man called Judas, located on the street called Straight. For three days he neither ate nor drank. He had plenty of time to think about his past actions. He recalled a man named Stephen, who had been stoned to death for preaching the Gospel. Saul had stood by, consenting to his death and, afterward launching his campaign of persecution of all the followers of "The Way". Now he prayed and repented of his deeds.

At end of three days, a man appeared at the door of Judas and asked to see Saul. His name was Ananias. The Lord had appeared to him in a vision, telling him to find Saul and minister to him. Ananias had, at first been reluctant, knowing Saul's reputation as a persecutor of the church, but finally relented and obeyed the Lord's command.

*And Ananias went his way, and entered into the house; and putting his hands on him said, Brother Saul, the Lord, even Jesus, that appeared unto thee in the way as thou camest, hath sent me, that thou mightest receive thy sight, and be filled with the Holy Ghost. And immediately there fell from his eyes as it had been scales: and he received sight forthwith, and arose, and was baptized.* (Acts 9:17-18)

Obeying the commission he had received from Jesus, Saul began to preach in the synagogues of Damascus, but persecution came to the persecutor. The Jews plotted to kill him, watching day and night for an opportunity to seize him. Their plans were thwarted, however, when some disciples took Saul and lowered him over the city wall by night. Saul went to Arabia for some time, exactly where is unknown. Some conjecture that he went to Sinai, but I think it was more likely the area of Petra, where he was taught by the Holy Spirit in preparation for becoming Christ's Apostle to the Gentiles.

After his stay in Arabia, Saul came back to Damascus and, later Jerusalem. He then traveled the known world, preaching the "good news" of the Gospel to the Gentiles, and was known by his Latin name, Paul. He wrote 13 epistles (letters), nearly one-fourth of the New Testament. Some scholars do not give him credit for the letter to the Hebrews, since his name is not included in the greeting. But judging from comments within the letter, I believe that he wrote it, also, making a total 14 letters. In his letter to the Christians at Corinth, he related the difficulties he endured for the Lord's sake:

*Thrice was I beaten with rods, once was I stoned, thrice I suffered shipwreck, a night and a day I have been in the deep; In journeyings often, in perils of waters, in perils of robbers, in perils by mine own countrymen, in perils by the heathen, in perils in the city, in perils in the wilderness, in perils in the sea, in perils among false brethren; In weariness and painfulness, in watchings often, in hunger and thirst, in fastings often, in cold and nakedness.* (2 Corinthians 11:25-27)

Near the end of his life, Paul summed up his ministry in his second letter to Timothy, as follows: " *I have fought a good fight, I have finished my course, I have kept the faith: Henceforth there is laid up for me a crown of righteousness, which the Lord, the righteous judge, shall give me at that day: and not to me only, but unto all them also that love his appearing".* (2 Timothy 4:7-8)

MILEPOSTS-

**The Transforming Power of the Gospel-** The life of Paul is testimony to the fact that God can take the worst sinner and make him into a faithful saint. When Jesus comes into a person's life, he will be changed. Have you allowed Him to change you?

**What Might You Accomplish-** if you submitted your life to Christ?

**Persecution-** At the Last Supper, Jesus prepared His disciples by telling them what they would suffer for His cause, *"They shall put you out of the synagogues: yea, the time cometh, that whosoever killeth you will think that he doeth God service."* (John 16:2). We are entering a time of persecution, in our day. Christians need to be ready to face whatever the world throws at us and remain faithful to Him.

**It is Worth it All-** Our Lord has promised to reward all who are faithful to Him. Paul said in one of his letters to the young Timothy, *"Henceforth there is laid up for me a crown of righteousness, which the Lord, the righteous judge, shall give me at that day: and not to me only, but unto all them also that love his appearing."* (2 Timothy 4:8)

# 21

# The Path Back to Paradise

*"In all thy ways acknowledge him, and he shall direct thy paths."* (Proverbs 3:6)

Four travelers paused to catch their breath at the crest of Mount Symbolum. They were 1600 feet above sea level and, looking back, could see the seaport of Neapolis, from which they had just come. Paul, Silas, Timothy and Luke were on their way to the city of Philippi. Only a few days before, they had sailed from Troas, in response to a vision in which a man had appeared to Paul and asked him to come over into Macedonia (a region of Greece) and help them. Now they were traveling overland by the Egnatian Way, a road built by Roman engineers, which was the main route across northern Greece. After resting from their climb, they began the descent down the other side of the mountain towards Philippi, one of the chief cities of the region. Philippi was a Roman colony and was the first place where Paul would preach the Gospel in Europe.

On the first Sabbath day after their arrival, they went out of the city to the riverside where local Jews worshipped, because there was no synagogue there.

There they met Lydia, a business woman who sold purple dye.

> *And a certain woman named Lydia, a seller of purple, of the city of Thyatira, which worshipped God, heard us: whose heart the Lord opened, that she attended unto the things which were spoken of Paul. And when she was baptized, and her household, she besought us, saying, If ye have judged me to be faithful to the Lord, come into my house, and abide there. And she constrained us.* (Acts 16:14-15)

Then, one day, a slave girl who was possessed by a demon, and was exploited by her masters in fortune telling, began to follow Paul and his friends. *"The same followed Paul and us, and cried, saying, These men are the servants of the most high God, which shew unto us the way of salvation."* (Acts 16:17). After several days of putting up with this, Paul decided to do something about it: *"Paul, being grieved, turned and said to the spirit, I command thee in the name of Jesus Christ to come out of her. And he came out the same hour.* (Acts 16:18) The slave girl's masters were very much displeased at this, because it meant they had lost a source of income. They seized Paul and dragged him before the local magistrates. Upon hearing their complaint, the magistrates had Paul and Silas beaten and thrown into prison.

Without a doubt, most people would be depressed at being beaten and thrown into prison, and wondering what else might happen to them. But Paul and Silas were not deterred. At midnight, they were praying and singing hymns to God, when an earthquake shook the foundations of the prison and all the doors were opened. The keeper of the prison, when he discovered what had happened, drew his sword and was about to kill himself because he thought all the prisoners had escaped.

*But Paul cried with a loud voice, saying, Do thyself no harm: for we are all here. Then he called for a light, and sprang in, and came trembling, and fell down before Paul and Silas, And brought them out, and said, Sirs, what must I do to be saved? And they said, Believe on the Lord Jesus Christ, and thou shalt be saved, and thy house. And they spake unto him the word of the Lord, and to all that were in his house. And he took them the same hour of the night, and washed their stripes; and was baptized, he and all his, straightway. And when he had brought them into his house, he set meat before them, and rejoiced, believing in God with all his house.* (Acts 16:28-34)

When day came, the magistrates sent for the officers and commanded them to let Paul and Silas go. Paul and Silas, however, were Roman citizens and were not about to leave quietly. Instead, Paul sent word that the magistrates had wrongfully treated them, as Roman citizens, and they would have to come and escort them out of the city. The magistrates came, apologized to them, and shamefacedly led them out of Philippi.

*The Path Back to Paradise*

MILEPOSTS-

**The Path of Mankind -** When Adam and Eve sinned by disobeying God and eating the forbidden fruit, they fell from the grace of God. Cast out of paradise, they began to walk on a path that all mankind has followed ever since. When we are born, we inherit their sinful nature and the natural thing for us to do is to continue in sin, walking ever further away from fellowship with our Creator. The end result is a tragic separation from God for eternity.

**The Path Back to Paradise -** Fortunately, there is another path we can walk, that leads back to fellowship with God and eternal life *"Jesus saith unto him, I am the way, the truth, and the life: no man cometh unto the Father, but by me."* (John 14:6)

**The Romans Road to Salvation -** Is a simple way of explaining the Good News of Salvation, using verses from the New Testament book of Romans:

**A**dmit you are a sinner in need of the Savior
*"For all have sinned, and come short of the glory of God"* (Romans 3:23)

**B**elieve that Jesus died to pay the penalty for your sins
*"But God commendeth his love toward us, in that, while we were yet sinners, Christ died for us."* (Romans 5:8)

**C**onfess Jesus as Lord and Savior of your life.
*"That if thou shalt confess with thy mouth the Lord Jesus, and shalt believe in thine heart that God hath*

*raised him from the dead, thou shalt be saved. For with the heart man believeth unto righteousness; and with the mouth confession is made unto salvation."* (Romans 10:9-10)

**Remember -**
1. God doesn't hate you. He hates your sin but He loves you
2. The Father loved you enough to send Jesus to redeem you
3. Jesus loved you enough to die on the cross for you
4. The invitation is to "whosoever"
5. When we respond in faith, we receive a new life that lasts forever

Amen

CPSIA information can be obtained at www.ICGtesting.com
Printed in the USA
BVOW080002121012

302792BV00001B/1/P